Measurement and Evaluation in Higher Education

Measurement and Evaluation in Higher Education:
Issues and Illustrations

by Thomas E Jordan

The Falmer Press
(A member of the Taylor & Francis Group)
London ● New York ● Philadelphia

UK   The Falmer Press, Falmer House, Barcombe, Lewes, East Sussex, BN8 5DL

USA   The Falmer Press, Taylor & Francis Inc., 242 Cherry Street, Philadelphia, PA 19106-1906

First published 1989

British Library Cataloguing in Publication Data

Jordan, Thomas E.
   Measurement and evaluation in higher education: issues and illustrations
   I. United States. Higher education. Assessment.
I. Title
378.73
ISBN 1 85000 575 3
ISBN 1 85000 576 1 (pbk.)

Jacket design by Caroline Archer

Typeset in 11/13 Bembo by
Alresford Typesetting & Design, Bramley, Basingstoke, Hants

Printed in Great Britain by Taylor & Francis (Printers) Ltd, Basingstoke

Contents

Acknowledgments

I wish to express my thanks to the following for permission to cite and to quote from copyrighted materials:

The evaluative criteria of the American Library Association which appeared in *C and RL News*, June, 1988 © 'Pathways for 1972 high school seniors', reprinted from HILTON, T.L. and SCHRADER, W.R. (1988) *Pathways to Graduate School: An Empirical Study Based on National Longitudinal Data*, Educational Testing Service (reprinted by permission). Materials in Chapter Five from *Colleges and University Business Administration* (1982) are reprinted by permission of the National Association of College and University Business Officers. I wish to thank the Council for the Advancement of Standards for Student Services for permission to reproduce materials; further information may be obtained from, CAS, Office of Students Affairs, University of Maryland, College Park, MD.

Preface

A little over 100 years ago, in 1860, a British politician in William Gladstone's Cabinet looked at state subsidy of education for the nation's children and reached a melancholy conclusion. Robert Lowe appraised the flow of money from the coffers of Threadneedle Street to the nascent system of elementary schooling and decided that money was being squandered (Briggs, 1954). In Gladstone's administration grants to local schools were cut back while, at the same time, the Benthamite cry of, 'payment for results' became the policy of Whitehall. Today, mutatis mutandis, we hear a similar call and public officials raise the Utilitarian's question of whether the electorate is getting what it pays for. In the current debate the question extends from elementary schools to higher education. Unlike previous revivals of attention the movement of the moment seems to be part of a wider questioning. Robert Lowe's successors in Whitehall have developed the Universities Funding Council (UFC) and proposed a radical shift in funding policy and practice for British higher education.

In the United States, for the first time, a generation is facing a phenomenon the rest of the countries of the world have known, the problem of failure. For some nations the last 1000 years have taught the same lesson to each generation, that failure is inevitable, and that the zeitgeist, or spirit of the times, needs to incorporate the hard-learned lessons of failure. To some contemporary Americans Vietnam represents a palpable failure in crusade which was morally an imperative; to others the experiences lacked justification, but for both the outcome was the same, a sense of failure. Two decades later, the self-estimated superiority in technology has vanished, and unemployment created by failure to compete successfully in the world economy rankles. At the same time, geopolitical forces in the form of the rise of militant Islam in the critical oil-producing portions of the Middle East has shown that two oceans offer little immunity from military-political hazards which the rest of the world has learned to live with over the centuries.

Assessment of the outcomes of higher education is an important topic for American education and for society in general. This large, expensive enterprise is viewed, as an article of faith, as the middle-class vehicle for vocational training, elevation of the sensibilities and for easing the transition from childhood to adulthood. However, the university is a perennial topic for critics; in *The Closing of the American Mind,* Bloom (1987) added to the list of complaints, beginning with the relativism which students bring to the campus. Bloom saw the university disintegrating, and considered the advent of the MBA degree as a 'disaster'. In some respects Bloom's jeremiad was prefigured in his citation of Plato's Republic as a text from which to approach contemporary higher education.

A rather different approach to knowledge, to *Cultural Literacy*, as Hirsch (1987) phrased it, removes knowledge from the context of learning as a process. Hirsch asserted that one need not be a mathematician to use the concepts of that admirable discipline. Inferentially, one need not employ the campus as a mediating concept to bring the inquiring mind to 'cultural literacy'. Hirsch ended *Cultural Literacy* with sixty-three pages of double-columned terms and concepts which are the concepts 'Every American needs to know'.

The two critiques are by no means bed-fellows; Bloom calls for reform of an agency of society, for cure of a social ill. In contrast, Hirsch addresses the remediable deficiencies of individuals. In these two critiques of the higher learning, echoing in some respects the views of Robert Hutchins, we see that the college curriculum has long been a topic for disputation and for complaints. At the moment, others are entering the arena, and the difference is less than it seems. The topic of assessment is current among university people and State legislators, and commands national audiences among those charged with carrying it out. As a problem area in higher education it is both obvious and subtle. On the one hand its importance is virtually self-evident, but on closer examination it turns out to be an intellectual complex with formidable technical and procedural problems. In one respect it is a repudiation of a major refinement in higher education which appears to have been uniquely American; that is, the emphasis on assessment of outcomes at the Baccalaureate level reverses the traditional de-emphasis of examinations as major events at wide intervals. To many students around the world, assessment is reduced to all-or-nothing evaluation, frequently viva voce, in which years of reading are assessed in a highly subjective manner in a context of great personal anxiety. In contrast, the typical American student has taken mid- and end-of-semester examinations, and has treated the final semester much like any other. Of course, there are exceptions, and some institutions require a major paper in the senior year, but they are a minority. This innovation of evaluating at the end of semesters or years had seemed enlightened in some other countries. For example, at Oxford Polytechnic in England two-thirds of the students choose to pursue degrees in American-style modules (Kiley, 1988). It may well be disconcerting to learn that the new is now evolving into something resembling the old in the trend of higher education. Assessment at the time of graduation through a comprehensive examination in the major field of study may be eroding a unique American pattern of assessment at the end of each course.

The current emphasis on assessment of outcomes follows a previous emphasis on evaluation of campus curricula and tables of organization. Many campuses engage continuously in review of their programs. Cycles of five years coincide from time to time with external processes of review for purposes of accreditation. In some instances, the process is confined to a single discipline when a professional school seeks to renew accreditation from, for example, the American Assembly of Collegiate Schools of Business. Another example is external appraisal by the State to accredit teacher education. The most comprehensive is appraisal for accreditation of the entire campus by (for example) the Middle States Association, the Southern States Association, or the largest of them all, the North Central Association of Colleges and Universities.

The new emphasis differs in some significant respects. It takes individual students as the module to be appraised, and some State governments seek to have every student tested at the time of graduation. At the moment, such assessment of outcomes is not a requirement for qualifying for a degree, but as States assert their control it seems imminent. An anomaly is that the public accepts sampling of behavior in other areas of life, for example, polling voters. It may be that as zeal is encapsuled by procedures campuses may not be required to test every student every year. That outcome is by no means certain, however.

In this work, I present the current range of issues in assessment of higher education. However, I do so from the position of one who is on campus. The consequence is that there are emphases, positive and negative, in the work which require an orientation to the text. I view State authority in public higher education to be a fact, but I prefer the perspective of the campus, the worms-eye view, in which the art of studying processes and outcomes is seen from within the instructional process. This point of view is broader than institutional research, and I introduce topics which represent a much wider point of view about the scope of assessment across the campus. It is for that reason that I present data from my own efforts to assess outcomes of learning in students in chapter 7. Accordingly, this book may be viewed as theory leavened by experience.

A word of caution is due; the illustrations, i.e. data from several hundred students, represent a tactical response to specific local circumstances. The value of the methods chosen may not be generalizable to all situations. The methods in question are statistical for the most part, and employ a multivariate technique of analysis whose illustrative value is its prime characteristic. There are other multivariate techniques and there are other ways to assess outcomes. The data represent my formulation of the theory, and of the politics, of assessment as a current theme of higher education. The presentation in chapter 7 is intended to show what one kind of evaluative data looks like, and to leaven an otherwise wholly theoretical presentation with concrete examples of data, statistical analysis and interpretations. By those items I wish to illustrate that the call to evaluate higher education demands a great deal from us, and in quite specific terms.

An additional point is that my illustrative data came from a particular type of institution. It is an urban, commuter campus which has a research ethos. The undergraduate student body is non-traditional with many first generation college students. The graduate student body is local, national and international — especially in the sciences. Accordingly, my data are site-specific, but all data are, unless we could draw on some yet-to-be executed regional or national study. In that respect these site-specific data are better than no data for a topic, evaluation in higher education, more typically discussed in terms of goals, and demands for accountability, than through actual data. The data will be presented in chapter 7; there, enough information is provided to illustrate aspects of evaluation. The reader who wishes a full presentation of the data may contact the author for a full set of figures and statistical analyses.

At the time of writing, assessment of higher education has a largely historic value as research workers scramble to translate direct orders into sound operations consistent with the university tradition of scientific scruples and honesty. Reconciliation of the external demand with the internal response is not easy. The external demand is in some respects a need which higher education might have addressed sooner. To have done so would have required a deeper appreciation of the fact that the contemporary *weltanschaung* of systems, of auditors as philosopher-kings, and fiscal conservatism were here to stay. The several states appear to have ended their honeymoon with higher education, a denouement imminent in student actions of the 1960s and early 1970s. Today's colleges are called to the bar of accountability and must make sure they are not found wanting.

I wish to express my thanks to the following for permission to reproduce materials: American Council on Education; National

Association of State Universities and Land Grant Colleges; Educational Testing Service, Inc.; Education Commission of the States; ERIC Clearing House on Higher Education; the Honorable John Ashcroft; Dr William Bennett; Dr Charles McClain; American Library Association; North Central Association of Schools and Colleges; Northwestern Association of Schools and Colleges; Western Association of Schools and Colleges; New England Association of Schools and Colleges; Middle States Association of Schools and Colleges; Southern Association of Schools and Colleges; Council for the Advancement of Student Services; National Association of College and University Business Officers; and Harper and Row, Inc.

Thomas E. Jordan
1989

Chapter 1

American Higher Education

In an age of nation-states with strong central governments and sophisticated means of communication it is an anomaly that American higher education is decentralized. Virtually all other countries approach higher education as a public matter to be governed by the central government. In contrast, the United States' Constitution of 1787 set the stage for diversified forms of public business. In consequence, higher education in the United States is heterogeneous, and it is sponsored by a variety of public, religious and non-sectarian bodies. In the western states, public higher education predominates, and elsewhere private education is a major component. The distinction between these two classes of education is blurred in the matter of funding as private institutions eagerly accept public money for student loans and for research. However, private institutions retain great flexibility which allows them to implement changes very rapidly.

In 1985/86 there were 12,247,055 persons enrolled in higher education according to the Digest of Educational Statistics (1988). Almost ten million of them were undergraduates and they enrolled in over 3000 institutions of higher learning (N = 3340). Of that number, half (N = 1622) were private non-profit institutions (48.6 per cent). Across the United States there are 883 colleges sponsored by the individual states. In towns across the country there are 794 religiously-sponsored colleges of which about two-thirds (N = 523) have Protestant bodies as sponsors. In recent decades, the fiscal linkages have softened and denominated colleges can no longer presume that a religious body will bail them out of financial problems. Neither public nor private colleges can look to the national government, and Washington has been retreating from direct support of higher education for many years. For private institutions, fees are a major source of income and are the counterpart to State allocations of funds as a major component of budget management. Both public and private institutions now pursue gift money in earnest. For both styles of higher education, demonstration of good management, which includes data on their effectiveness based on student achievement and attitudes, is vital to soliciting gift money from individual donors and large corporations.

When we examine the nation's colleges and universities through table 1 we see that virtually all are coeducational and one-third offer less than four years of work; usually, they are styled Junior or Community Colleges. Most of the rest offer Bachelor's and Master's degrees, and about one in six or seven offers Doctorates also. From the point of view of assessing outcomes, it is apparent that the goals and accomplishments should vary by the nature of the institutions. The mission of a Community College tends to be vocational or to provide two years of general education for students seeking Baccalaureate degrees. Such institutions tend to have virtually open admission. Assessment in that context must take into account the level of academic preparation in entrants, their range of goals, and the question of whether they are full- or part-time students.

In the four-year's-plus-Master's institutions most of the items just listed also prevail, plus the additional matter of selectivity of admission, and whether students are in residence or commute. For some undergraduates, the goal is to earn the first degree and get a job, while for others the goal is to enter graduate or professional schools. In the case of some Baccalaureate programs there is a barrier to entrance to be surmounted by good grades at the end of the second year of study. Some students transfer-in to enter a program in the third, junior, year, while others transfer-out and enroll in programs only available on another campus. Assessment in that context faces the question of still more diversity in campus mission, and in students' private career objectives.

In the case of doctoral-level institutions, their distinctive offerings are not a large proportion of the curriculum and so evaluation and assessment resembles that in less comprehensive settings, for the most part. The exceptions are the award to doctoral recipients of post-doctoral fellowships, in the sciences especially, as an index of quality. A second element is the importance of attracting research funds in order to conduct research and to provide fiscal support for PhD aspirants. Absence of research funding places PhD programs at a serious disadvantage in universities where campus support is less than first rate. The fact is that the best students are competed for; external research funds plus campus funds ensure enrollment of the best graduate students, and so raise the quality of graduate life.

The preceding comment applies in some respects to all levels of college instruction, and a bright student body exists only as a result of effective strategies to enroll bright undergraduates. Assessment of colleges includes scrutiny of their scholarship and recruiting activities.

Private Higher Education

The existence of colleges and universities sponsored by agencies other than the national or local government is a distinctive feature of American higher education. The private institutions parallel all but the largest public institutions and systems of institutions in many respects. That is, their quality ranges from competitive in international comparisons to third rate and probably a scandal. A distinctive quality emerging from the comparative lack of governmental control is the freedom to innovate in providing curricula. Programs can be started — and closed — in a fashion quite sensitive to local or national clienteles. Accordingly, innovative programming is a criterion of quality for the assessment of outcomes. Graduates should be superior as a result of greater institutional freedom to modify curricula. Of course, the curricular challenge is to distinguish a fad from a trend, but career opportunities emerge and curricula should respond to new job descriptions evolved from traditional formulations.

Urban Higher Education

American society is structured at several points by the formative experience of the nineteenth century. In that mode, education was left to private sponsorship, primarily, above the high school level. In the 1920s some cities established their own colleges, but some states were slow to provide higher education for their urban residents. The result is that today's newer urban campuses face interesting opportunities. In the view of Arnold Grobman (1988), the rural land-grant tradition of the Morrill Act of 1862 has given way to the urban grant university as the frontier of opportunity. In Marguerite R. Barnett's view (1988) urban public universities face three challenges, 'to respond creatively to the decline of urban school systems', to 'prepare students for an economy that requires mathematics and science literacy', and to 'provide assistance to emergent, research-based or knowledge-based prototype firms'.

Public Higher Education

A distinctive aspect of American higher education is the responsibility which the fifty states assume for public higher education. In a truly unique

Table 1: Institutions of higher education and branches, by control of institution, highest level of offering, and sex of student body, 1985–86

Highest level of offering and sex of student body	Total	Public					Private				
		Federal[1]	State	Local (city, county, or district)	State and local	State-related	Independent non-profit	Organized as profit-making	Religious group		
									Protestant	Catholic	Other[2]
All institutions	3,340	13	883	173	398	31	828	220	524	235	35
Coeducational	3,126	13	881	173	398	31	726	218	505	168	13
Men only	99	0	1	0	0	0	47	0	3	30	18
Women only[3]	102	0	1	0	0	0	48	2	14	34	3
Coordinate[3]	13	0	0	0	0	0	7	0	2	3	1
Less than 4 years beyond high school	1,309	3	356	170	383	20	121	190	43	20	3
Coeducational	1,282	3	356	170	383	20	107	188	40	13	2
Men only	6	0	0	0	0	0	4	0	0	2	0
Women only	20	0	0	0	0	0	9	2	3	5	1
Coordinate[3]	1	0	0	0	0	0	1	0	0	0	0
4 or 5-year baccalaureate degree	707	5	73	1	5	2	242	19	286	70	4
Coeducational	627	5	72	1	5	2	209	19	275	37	2
Men only	31	0	1	0	0	0	10	0	2	16	2
Women only	46	0	0	0	0	0	22	0	8	16	0
Coordinate[3]	3	0	0	0	0	0	1	0	1	1	0
First-professional degree	93	0	9	0	0	0	67	2	11	2	2
Coeducational	80	0	9	0	0	0	58	2	10	1	0
Men only	12	0	0	0	0	0	9	0	0	1	2
Women only	1	0	0	0	0	0	0	0	1	0	0
Coordinate[3]	0	0	0	0	0	0	0	0	0	0	0

Master's degree	566	2	148	1	0	3	196	5	103	105	3
Coeducational	525	2	148	1	0	3	181	5	100	82	3
Men only	12	0	0	0	0	0	4	0	0	8	0
Women only	24	0	0	0	0	0	9	0	2	13	0
Coordinate[3]	5	0	0	0	0	0	2	0	1	2	0
Beyond master's but less than doctorate	153	0	100	0	4	0	25	0	13	9	2
Coeducational	146	0	100	0	4	0	22	0	13	7	0
Men only	5	0	0	0	0	0	1	0	0	2	2
Women only	2	0	0	0	0	0	2	0	0	0	0
Coordinate[3]	0	0	0	0	0	0	0	0	0	0	0
Doctorate	473	3	197	1	6	6	153	1	68	29	9
Coeducational	462	3	196	1	6	6	148	1	67	28	6
Men only	4	0	0	0	0	0	0	0	1	1	2
Women only	3	0	1	0	0	0	2	0	0	0	0
Coordinate[3]	4	0	0	0	0	0	3	0	0	0	1
Undergraduate nondegree-granting	15	0	0	0	0	0	11	1	0	0	3
Coeducational	2	0	0	0	0	0	1	1	0	0	0
Men only	7	0	0	0	0	0	6	0	0	0	1
Women only	6	0	0	0	0	0	4	0	0	0	2
Coordinate[3]	0	0	0	0	0	0	0	0	0	0	0
Graduate nondegree-granting	22	0	0	0	0	0	13	0	0	0	9
Coeducational	0	0	0	0	0	0	0	0	0	0	0
Men only	22	0	0	0	0	0	13	0	0	0	9
Women only	0	0	0	0	0	0	0	0	0	0	0
Coordinate[3]	0	0	0	0	0	0	0	0	0	0	0

[1]Includes ten US Service Schools, Haskell Indian Junior College, Institute of American Indian Arts and Oglala Sioux Community College.
[2]Includes Jewish, Latter-Day Saints, Greek Orthodox, Russian Orthodox and Unitarian.
[3]Institutions with separate colleges for men and women.
Source: US Department of Education, Center for Education Statistics, 'Institutional Characteristics of Colleges and Universities, 1985–86' survey.

manner the states tax themselves to provide higher education; funds from the national government are not available for the general support of campuses, but only for specific programs. For the fifty states, the proportion of State budget allocated to higher education in 1982/83 ranged from 14.7 per cent in Arizona to 4.8 per cent in Massachusetts. Since states vary in population and wealth, percentages of gross expenditures on public affairs can be misleading, however. At 10.4 per cent, California is not as generous, proportionately, as Arizona, but the amount of money in dollars is enormous and supports 137 campuses.

Accordingly, it is not unreasonable that expenditure of State government funds on higher education has led, in recent years, to calls for more accountability and for assessment of what the quality of the product is. With the evident slow-up in the public's willingness to be taxed further, the alternative has been to raise the efficiency of the available resources. The question of what the public gets for its higher education investment is fair. The public has a right to know that its satisfaction with higher education is justified. The average person is a careful consumer and can reasonably ask if, as a consumer of college offerings, value is received. The answer is that value is received by the taxpayer or consumer, but demonstrating that outcome is a matter of interest and of complexity.

To begin with there is the sheer scope of public higher education in some states. California has 137 campuses supported by the State's budget. At the other extreme, Wyoming has eight small campuses, and the largest, in Laramie, has about 10,000 students. Vermont has only six public campuses, but there are also sixteen private colleges to serve the population. When there are many campuses to review, states tend

Table 2: State tax fund appropriations for operating expenses of higher education for +scal years 1978–79, 1986–87 and 1988–89, with percentages of gain over the most recent two and ten years (in thousand of dollars).

States	Year 1978–79	Year 1986–87	Year 1988–89	2-yr gain Per cent	10-yr gain Per cent
(1)	(2)	(3)	(4)	(5)	(6)
Alabama	328,494	632,054	763,000	21	132
Alaska	84,593	208,356	164,733	− 21	95
Arizona	218,166	450,681	544,560	21	150
Arkansas	140,319	270,530	286,399	6	104
California	2,344,345	4,507,731	5,011,510	11	114
Colorado	237,310	423,132	475,181	12	100
Connecticut	206,901	384,589	467,385	22	126
Delaware	48,831	96,797	107,516	11	120
Florida	535,809	1,278,584	1,474,345	15	175
Georgia	346,731	714,004	812,299	14	134

Hawaii	113,767	220,845	274,233	24	141
Idaho	83,322	126,030	144,987	15	74
Illinois	845,579	1,391,996	1,399,444	1	66
Indiana	369,308	661,635	755,614	14	105
Iowa	275,065	404,701	478,991	18	74
Kansas	222,216	325,725	382,326	17	72
Kentucky	272,909	458,968	518,361	13	90
Louisiana	278,169	499,569	483,034	– 3	74
Maine	49,047	125,701	162,432	29	231
Maryland	292,755	569,975	695,261	22	137
Massachusetts	273,333	816,374	868,426	6	218
Michigan	733,978	1,225,522	1,338,033	9	82
Minnesota	433,761	782,471	861,462	10	99
Mississippi	218,950	326,353	425,751	30	94
Missouri	284,836	476,420	550,609	16	93
Montana	55,050	101,187	105,277	4	91
Nebraska	140,538	215,234	253,431	18	80
Nevada	50,112	102,419	121,249	18	142
New Hampshire	27,542	55,961	72,454	29	163
New Jersey	442,277	893,549	1,129,452	26	155
New Mexico	119,474	250,719	268,800	7	125
New York	1,421,407	2,770,779	3,110,021	12	119
North Carolina	521,863	1,172,120	1,329,606	13	155
North Dakota	61,747	120,472	118,072	– 2	91
Ohio	604,651	1,208,155	1,320,460	9	118
Oklahoma	196,595	383,690	415,191	8	111
Oregon	204,000	335,998	361,189	7	77
Pennsylvania	697,987	1,105,210	1,268,759	12	77
Rhode Island	68,972	117,479	138,802	18	101
South Carolina	265,076	504,124	576,598	14	118
South Dakota	47,466	72,214	77,369	7	63
Tennessee	312,799	615,764	673,881	9	115
Texas	1,042,243	1,967,184	2,245,958	14	115
Utah	132,524	244,386	259,615	6	96
Vermont	25,509	46,083	53,855	17	11 i
Virginia	425,797	902,068	1,033,096	15	143
Washington	382,750	628,981	719,437	14	88
West Virginia	148,249	241,865	252,618	4	70
Wisconsin	433,482	666,525	738,670	11	70
Wyoming	47,043	114,188	114,753	0	144
Totals	17,113,647	32,215,097	36,204,505		
Weighted average percentages of gain				12	111

Source: Hines, R.R. *Appropriations of State Tax Funds for Operating Expenses of Higher Education.* Washington, DC. National Association of State Universities and Land Grant Colleges, 1989.

to decentralize assessment and require summaries. Where governors' personal interest is high, states tend to be more formal in their expectations. In the mid–eighties, Florida, New Jersey, Tennessee and Missouri were such states and placed explicit requirements on public campuses for reports of undergraduate achievement in the major field of study at the point of graduation. Such requirements are understandable, but they are expensive to execute and the campus dollar can be spent only once. The cost in time and manpower does not vitiate the call to accountability in a rational system of State spending. It seems only a quid pro quo, however, that State plans be equally accountable and open to public scrutiny.

It is salutary to consider the nature of an item to be evaluated before evaluating it. The overall impression one gains of higher education in the United States is diversity. It is big, it is geographicaly dispersed and quality varies from place to place. The very best is quite recognizable, in the form of ratings by more than 1000 college Presidents, Deans and admissions officers surveyed by *U.S. News and World Report* (America's Best Colleges, 1988). The ten best national universities, in order, were: Yale, Princeton, California, Harvard, Massachusetts, Stanford, Dartmouth, Columbia, Rice and Chicago. The ten best national liberal arts colleges were: Swarthmore, Amherst, Williams, Wellesley, Pomona, Wesleyan, Smith, Grinnell, Bowdoin and Haverford. The ten best small, comprehensive colleges were: Berea, Illinois Wesleyan, Alfred, Whittier, St Michael's, St Mary's, Beaver, Messiah, Moravian and LeMoyne. Given that there are over 3000 institutions of higher education it is understandable that being the best is necessarily the best with regard to several criteria of separate but equal validity.

However, all American colleges and universities share some things in common. We start to understand the similarities by recognizing that American higher education is fairly continuous with education from kindergarten to grade 12. In other countries, higher education has maintained a degree of separation from elementary and secondary education. The origins of that separation have usually been social, and intellectual, and the degree of separation has been a source of satisfaction to higher education when it prevails. Historically, higher education was for the economic élite, and élites tend to preserve their position with tenacity. At the same time, intellectual content rose and fell in previous centuries.

Peter the Great's first institution had no Russian students and he imported them from Germany. In Britain, entrance requirements in the nineteenth century were linked reciprocally to the curriculum of the public schools, and the connection persists (Jordan, 1987a). In the United States the founders of Harvard College intended to produce Divines to provide religious instruction. Until quite recently, higher education was viewed as inherently unsuitable for the working class, a view firmly squelched by those who took advantage of the G.I. Bill after World War II. Today, the gap between the twelfth grade and college entry has been largely erased and replaced by a deliberate process of transition. Selected high school students can take courses for college credit, and colleges trawl the ranks of high school students in order to recruit the talented. The relevance of this to our major theme is that the success of the best students graduating from college may have its origins in the pre-collegiate years. When the discreteness of the high school/college boundary is replaced by a more continuous process the accountability of colleges may merge with that of secondary schools to a degree. In that formulation college outcomes are cumulative; of course, that is not to carry the point to extremes and blame kindergarten for poor outcomes at the end of college. However, in 1988 the Congressional Office of Technology Assessment produced the report, *Educating Scientists and Engineers Grade School to Grad School* (Chubin, 1988). The title of that comprehensive study prefaced an examination of the educational origins of engineers and scientists. The study reported that it was in elementary school, or shortly after, that many vocational choices crystallized. The report described elementary school as, 'shaping the talent pool', and discussed the role of out-of-school experiences in shaping career interests and vocations. Presumably, young students who have made at least preliminary vocational choices select appropriate secondary school courses.

In 1987, Missouri began a program in which 15,000 students in secondary schools were tracked in order to assess the consequences of high school preparation on college success. The State's Coordinating Board for Higher Education formulated the essential college preparatory curriculum for secondary education as:

Four years of English
Three years of mathematics
Three years of social studies
Two years of natural science
Two years of foreign language

In the first year of tracking the impact of using and not using the recommended curriculum, Missouri learned that less than 25 per cent of the students under scrutiny had entered college with the degree of preparation recommended. The consequences of this were evident in the Freshmen year grades at four-year colleges, with those well-prepared receiving a mean grade higher by 0.3, at 2.7 on a four-point scale. An

Figure 1: *James Madison High School: A curriculum for American students* (Former educational secretary Bennett's proposed education model)

Subject	First Year	Second Year	Third Year	Fourth Year
English	Introduction to Literature: Homer's *Odyssey*, the Bible, Shakespeare, *Huckleberry Finn*, Dickens	American literature: Hawthorne, Poe, Whitman, Melville, Hemingway, Emerson	British literature: from Chaucer to Milton to T.S. Eliot to Shaw	Introduction to world literature: Greek and Roman classics, Dante, Cervantes, Ibsen, Dostoevsky, Zola, Mann
Social Studies	Western civilization	American history	Principles of American democracy (1 semester) and American democracy and the world (1 semester)	Elective
Math	Three years required from among the following courses: Algebra I, Plane and Solid Geometry, Algebra II and Trigonometry, Statisitics and Probability (1 semester), Pre-Calculus (1 semester) and Calculus AB or BC			Elective
Science	Three years required from among the following courses: Astronomy/Geology, Biology, Chemistry, and Physics or Principles of Technology			Elective
Foreign Language	Two years required in a single language from among offerings determined by local jurisdictions		Elective	Elective
Physical Education/ Health	Physical Education/ Health 9	Physical Education/ Health 10	Elective	Elective
Fine Arts	Art History (1 semester) Music History (1 semester)	Elective	Elective	Elective

interesting instance of the transition topic previously mentioned is that the Missouri Coordinating Board sent the Freshmen year grades to the high schools for their examination. By closing the information loop, going back to the high schools, the Coordinating Board hoped to stimulate a stronger course of study before young people enter college. Obviously, colleges would benefit from taking in young people whose previous schooling had been shaped towards the college experience. This innovation illustrates the point that effects in human development are the consequence of more than immediate and current influences. Some colleges have been slow to reject ill-prepared applicants, and young people have found that some college, somewhere, would accept them. Adolescent culture, ever ready for the easier way, has incorporated the pragmatic reality of virtually non-existent minimums into their secondary curricula, when allowed to do so by lax school boards.

In 1987, Ravitch and Finn reported the results of testing the knowledge of 7812 17-year-olds. In *What Do Our Seventeen-Year-Olds Know*, they report the outcomes of putting 141 history and 121 literature questions to youngsters in a sample representative of the entire national population; i.e., 12.9 per cent black and 28 per cent for the central states; 6.2 per cent attended Catholic schools. In history, Ravitch and Finn reported that the average history question was answered correctly by 54.5 per cent of the students. That phenomenon led Ravitch and Finn to summarize by saying, 'The students' overall performance is extremely weak'. On twelve map questions only 63.8 per cent of girls, 44.2 per cent of black students and 54.2 per cent of Hispanic students could locate Great Britain. In literature the performance was lower, and 51.8 per cent supplied correct answers. They went on to add that the literature curriculum has less coherence across the land than the history. Boys exceeded girls on history questions, and girls were higher on literature questions. The performance of students rose as their parents' education rose, and declined as they watched more TV. Ravitch and Finn concluded that the younger generation, '. . . is ignorant of important things that it should know, and that it and generations to follow are at risk of being gravely handicapped by that ignorance upon entry into adulthood, citizenship, and parenthood' (p. 201). It goes without saying that their college instructors, one year later, would have to cope with the 'generation at risk'.

In 1987, Secretary of Education William J. Bennett proposed that high school students take:

Four years of English
Three years of mathematics

Figure 2: *Pathways for 1972 high-school seniors: estimated number per 1000 sample members (actual N = 16,740)*

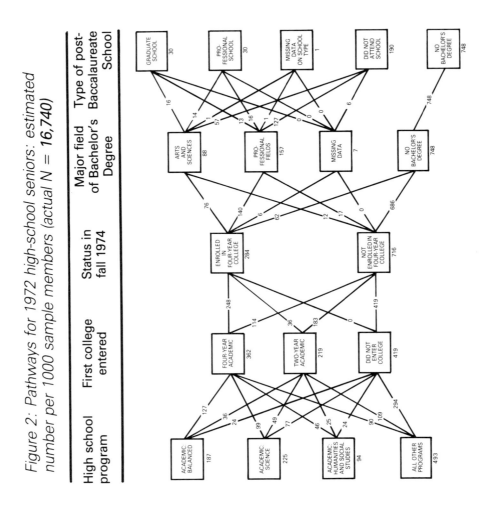

Three years of social studies
Two years of a foreign language
Two years of physical education
One semester of art history
One semester of music history

Also, in 1987, he proposed the model secondary school curriculum presented in figure 1. Its objective was to produce a well-educated adolescent. In curriculum making there is no end to the number of possible universal remedies. Dr Bennett's proposed curriculum conveys that determinacy may be demonstrated by considering figure 2, taken from the national longitudinal study of the high school class of 1972. The schema in figure 2 was derived from data gathered from a national sample of approximately 22,500 high school seniors who were surveyed every two years until 1979. The investigators, Thomas L. Hilton and William B. Schrader (1988), observed that

> By 1979, 3 per cent of the 1972 high school seniors had enrolled full time in graduate school, and 3 per cent had enrolled full time in professional school.
>
> Students reaching graduate or professional school tended to enroll in more demanding high school academic programs and were noticeably more likely to enroll first in four-year colleges after high school graduation.
>
> The distribution of males and females in the pathways and their educational attainment were similar, except that appreciably fewer females enrolled in professional schools.
>
> Almost as high a proportion of black students as of white students enrolled initially in four-year colleges, but a lower proportion received bachelor's degrees.
>
> Students reaching graduate school tended to show approximately the same pattern of choices as students reaching professional schools; the professional school students had somewhat higher test scores and educational aspirations, although the differences were small.
>
> Many uncertainties precluded predictions about their absolute numbers, but it is likely that the proportion of future post-Baccalaureate students who are female and the proportions from minority populations will be appreciably higher.

Another aspect of American higher education is the infusion of a major social agenda, the expansion of opportunity for all peoples. Under that rubric, colleges have shifted from a passive role in which they hoped talented minorities would apply to aggressive programs of recruiting in which students of ability are identified quite early and then tracked for possible recruitment much as high school athletes were, and are, scouted. The consequence of this broadening of opportunity is that entering college students lack the homogeneity of former generations. That is, they no longer present uniform personal characteristics such as a family tradition of going to college, or of widespread travel, and so find campuses rather impersonal, alien places. To some entering students, a campus library is an incredible place because they have only known a small room with few books as a library. Similarly, the middle-class culture of campus life and modes of conduct can be novel and anxiety-producing. The sheer diversity of people on a campus can be amazing to students whose previous contacts have been within one ethnic group. The presence of students from Asia and the Middle East, for example, can be hard to assimilate. Even Middle America's young people can seem exotic, and regional accents can be a hindrance to learning.

For the purpose of this review, the significance lies in the historical trend away from homogeneity of backgrounds, and therefore of expectations for the outcomes of the college experience. At one time the degree was the hoped-for outcome and, secondarily, a marketable credential or skill in some cases, but not all. With the shift to heterogeneity we see a cultural lag; it is evident in the accent on vocationalism evident in current enrollments in schools of business and the decline in interest in sociology and the non-applied disciplines. In contrast, colleges still have their faculties in fields where demand has dried up, if only temporarily. Faculties control curricula and their formulation of outcomes tends to be in quite traditional, non-trendy terms. Obviously, faculties eventually adjust their sense of priorities, and they do so while also accommodating students from backgrounds with which they are unfamiliar. This creates an inevitable discrepancy except in those instances where faculties have consciously deliberated and developed statements of policy about the outcomes they wish the curriculum to produce. Such statements are broader than they used to be and convey a sense of traditionalism modulated by vocationalism.

At the level of structure, a third element is that American higher education is not a public utility owned and operated by the nation-state. A consequence of a written constitution is that the fifty states exercise the functions not explicitly assigned in 1787 to the national government. In the context of a world of local process, intended to avoid centralized authority whenever possible, the fifty states provide higher education as well as elementary and secondary education. Of course, the views of 1787 have evolved, and higher education derives support, and a concomitant degree of control, from the Federal government. A prime example at the moment is the way in which higher education accounts for Federal funds for research under the Federal Office of Management and Budget's regulation A-21. However, the initiative still lies with the states. Most of them have developed powerful, legislatively authorized bureaucracies to guide the expansion of higher education, to monitor quality and to advise legislators on budgetary matters. The result is a complex pattern of higher education. In some states the process is not far advanced, while in others, California being the prime example, higher education consists of elaborate structures ranging from community colleges with open admission policies to campuses open only to the academic élite. From this breadth, we infer an equal breadth of intended outcomes, and we see that assessment addresses quite different matters from campus to campus, but also from state to state. This last point is important because state governors have been leaders in recent years in the search for ways to assess the outcomes of higher education. Their motivation has been the reasonable expectation that there be an accounting of the results which public generosity has permitted. It is in part fiscal accountancy, while also addressing the management of resources in an age when considerable sophistication is the standard for relating budgeting to programming. In table 2 is a list of state allocations for higher education. It should be kept in mind that these public monies are supplemented by fee income and by grants and contracts. The result is a larger budget for states' higher education than is evident in the allocations in table 2.

A distinctive feature of American higher education is its diversity. In the matrix of traits the public-private aspect of colleges is uniquely American. The public institutions are dependents of governmental units. Cities sometimes sponsored colleges, for example, New York and Oklahoma City, but virtually all city colleges were taken over by State government when urban finances entered crises, so that State government tends to be the public sponsor of higher education. The usual pattern is for a governor to appoint people to the Board of Governors who supervise a college or, increasingly, several colleges judged to be similar. A fine point, but one which can have potentials for tension, is that some State universities are named in nineteenth century State constitutions, while more recent campuses tend to owe their existence to legislative authority. In the last analysis funds are recommended by legislatures to governors, so that the Golden Rule—'he that has the gold makes the rules'—tends to overcome the legal niceties.

Much of the pattern of public higher education sponsored by State governments was established in the nineteenth century. Typically, there was a State university placed like the asylum and the prison at a distance from the centers of population. In the jousting of the era each city got one public facility, and the debate over who was the winner and who the loser has never quite been settled. In addition, teachers colleges were established to normalize (standardize) instruction for the public schools. In the 1950s many of them made the transition from single to multi-purpose missions (Harcleroad and Ostar, 1987). Historically, the State universities have had great influence through the presence in State legislatures of graduates of the law schools on the campuses established first. Today, the tensions tend to be between country campuses and urban campuses, and the trend to increasing influence by urban legislators is evident. Such people bring a fairly applied view to the question of the outcomes of higher education. They see vocationalism as most important, and frequently relate the value of the urban campus to the economic future of the urban area.

Another form of tension is that between the applied and non-applied. In Great Britain, there has emerged the theme of 'enterprise', a term meant to convey that students can develop a sense of initiative in courses nominally far removed from applications. Enterprise is exemplified by learning to plan, to organize and to work in a team. Such traits can be acquired, it was argued by the government's Training Commission, when learning archaeology in the field through problem-solving and learning to use personal computers (Broom, 1988).

Still another type of tension is that between State government and public higher education. Newman (1987) addressed the topic in, *Choosing Quality: Reducing Conflict Between the State and the University*. In that work, Newman recommended eight items by which universities could move towards a positive relationship with state government and toward achievement of higher quality:

1 The university must have a sense of its niche; its particular role among other institutions of higher education, its particular programs and characteristics in which it will be outstanding. It must focus its resources on these areas and recognize that no university ever moved to greatness by trying to be everything to everybody. It will not spend its resources where it does not aspire to greatness.

2 While it must succeed at the task of research and graduate education, it must also devote the energy to excel at undergraduate education.

3 The university must create a climate that will attract a president, deans, faculty and students of high quality. It must be a place where people of diverse backgrounds involve themselves in teaching and learning, research and scholarship with the shared expectation of high standards. But the expectation of high standards must not stifle the taking of risk

and the exploration of new ideas. So the university must be supportive — at all levels — of carefully thought-out risk-taking.

4 The university must move to ensure freedom for all points of view on campus, first by restating clearly and unequivocally the responsibility of the university to be open to all views, including the unpopular, and then by acting to exercise that right and responsibility so that it does not wither.

5 Campus leadership must have the courage to set standards, evaluate results, eliminate outmoded or ineffective programs and search relentlessly for ways to improve.

6 The university must take those actions that are needed and responsible so that state frustration does not lead to inappropriate actions. Academics need to remember that, left without a solution to a pressing problem, the political system will create one.

7 The essential exercise of institutional striving must take place within a clearly understood mission that is shared with the board and the state, and must avoid constant attempts to subvert that mission for reasons of self-interest.

8 The university must take the state leadership seriously, must recognize that the state has legitimate interests and an important role in higher education. It must understand the needs of the state and work diligently at adapting the university to help achieve these.

Previously, the role of the national government has been touched on. While it is true that there is no national university in the United States, it is also true that the Federal government operates many institutions of higher education. To begin with, there are the service academies to train officers for the Army, Navy and Air Force. Within each service there are vast educational enterprises. An example is the Command and General Staff College (CGSC) at Fort Leavenworth, Kansas. This is the agency through which captains go from all branches of the army — doctors to engineers — in a normalizing experience. This College is accredited like any other college, in this case by the North Central Association of Colleges and Universities. There is a civilian board of review which annually inspects the College and writes an annual report to the Secretary of the Army. CGSC awards a Master's degree to students who take a second year of study and write a thesis.

In the case of the military colleges, the question of accountability takes the form of providing satisfactory officers. Such people should be able to relate the current state of knowledge to their career specialities. The criterion of battles won is not measurable under normal circumstances. However, it illustrates a point about evaluation; that is, not every criterion is measurable on the day a person graduates. We turn, frequently, to the more readily measurable, but not always with an appreciation that such outcomes are convenient but not always the most relevant.

The military service is also connected through the Reserve Officers Training Corps (ROTC) which is found on many campuses. This is a mechanism by which undergraduates can finance their education in return for a limited period of service after graduation in one of the services. ROTC provides a second point at which the resources of the national government support the financing of higher education. For the ROTC, the pay-off is a person who is fit to receive a reserve commission and to play a useful role as a military officer. An accounting graduate who can help the Air Force manage its payroll is a highly explicit outcome.

Campus Factors Affecting Student Outcomes

In table 3 we present comparative international data on students' preparation in English and mathematics. Those numbers are correct, but it should be pointed out that tertiary education is more continuous with secondary education in the United States than elsewhere. For some students college means a daily trip to a large complex of buildings which resembles their high school. They live at home and play the role within the family they had previously known with, perhaps, a little more latitude. In a study of part-time students the Carnegie Foundation (1986) reported that such students were less likely to perceive faculty as helpful people, and experienced less of a sense of community on campus. For other students the transition may not be intellectually broad, but it is probably a major social transition to begin dormitory life, with assumption of full responsibility for independent living. The success with which students integrate new ways of behaving and of meeting responsibility is a major influence on academic success. Higher SAT scores may be less important than prior experiences away from home in determining responsiveness to the academic program. Accordingly, the outcomes of the college experience can be influenced positively and negatively by the impact of the campus as a social organization.

Social Considerations

The size of a campus and its architecture create an atmosphere which is perceived as warm and supportive or as large, cold and impersonal.

Commuter campuses tend to plan for time in classrooms but offer little beyond the library or cafeteria between classes. What tends to be ignored is provision for private space analogous to the dormitory room or apartment to which the residential student retreats during the day. Campus life requires time outside of classrooms and a large, welcoming student center can do much to provide support and companionship. In its absence, even bright, well-prepared students may feel alienated.

For some students life on a commuter or residential campus may provide the first exposure to people from other religious and ethnic groups. Sometimes young people have a family tradition of enrollment in college, and are prepared for diversity. For others preparation may consist of warnings about threats to their moral, political and religious values. Somewhere between these extremes the typical college student finds the college years broadening and informative outside the classroom. Occasionally, students find the apparent purposefulness of other students a contrast to their own lives, a conviction only partially correct, as they swim in a sea of faces and stand in lines. To other students the impersonal world of crowded sidewalks and unfamiliar people appears to be a deliberately hostile environment aimed at them personally. Clearly, matching student and campus, if at all possible, is vital to a successful college experience. Students with limited and limiting backgrounds can misperceive the style of a campus and find it threatening when it is merely different from their own parochial experience. In terms of assessing outcomes, the implication is that a student ill-at-ease on campus may not stick around long enough to be broadened and desensitized. In that respect, retention rates for Freshmen in the first semester may be as important as the performance of seniors on the Graduate Record Examination.

Academic Considerations

On the presumption that most students make a satisfactory adjustment to campus life we can turn to academic aspects of the college experience. This is the element which the faculty consider important, although not to the exclusion of social considerations.

The qualilty of instruction for undergraduates is accepted by faculties as a major responsibility. The process by which the most junior instructors are prepared to teach is less random than it used to be. Today, departments tend to prepare their teaching assistants for classroom leadership, and monitor their performance. In some fields few American students choose to enroll for graduates studies, preferring to go into jobs which pay well

Table 3: Average achievement score on an international test in algebra and calculus taken by advanced mathematics students in the 12th grade or equivalent in participating developed countries: 1982

| Country or province | Percentage of age group in advanced mathematics classes | Mathematics Achievement Scores | | | |
| | | For advanced mathematics students | | For top 5% of group (estimate) | |
		Algebra	Calculus	Algebra	Calculus
Belgium					
Flemish	10	51.3	49.8	57.5	55.6
French	10	48.0	47.9	55.3	53.7
Canada					
British Columbia	30	45.1	39.8	60.9	51.8
Ontario	19	48.7	49.4	59.6	59.4
England and Wales	6	52.3	53.6	54.9	56.1
Finland	15	53.0	52.7	60.7	61.0
Hungary	50	43.8	41.8	60.9	57.7
Japan	12	57.1	57.6	63.7	66.5
New Zealand	11	49.0	50.8	56.8	57.7
Scotland	18	45.7	44.6	56.2	52.9
Sweden	12	49.9	51.4	58.5	59.2
United States	13	43.7	43.2	52.8	50.9

Source: Miller, D. and Linn, R.L. (1986) 'Cross national achievement with differential retention rates', unpublished contractor report prepared for the US Department of Education, Center for Statistics, April, special tabulations.
Source: 'The Condition of Education' 1986.

initially. As a consequence, many graduate assistantships are taken up by, for example, Chinese and Indian students. In the case of Indian teaching assistants they may have been reading and writing English since their elementary school days. Their syntax is excellent, but their spoken English could be hard to comprehend for a student who has heard only one dialect of English. Currently, many colleges address the understandability of teaching assistants in formal, mandatory programs of evaluation and preparation. In fairness it should be appreciated that oral dialects are a broader problem than the non-native speakers of English. There are occasional instances of complaints in which the foreign instructor happens to come from another region of the United States. In either case, outcomes of college instruction depend on students' comprehension of their instructors and it is vital that college instructors be understood.

Another aspect of instruction is the use of large lecture halls and their unavoidable impersonality. In the best arrangements, students are organized into small sections which come together for lectures in a large auditorium. The degree of success realized in this cost-effective pattern of instruction goes a long way to influencing students' sense of alienation or enthusiasm. In some respects the diffusion of computer terminals across campus is a related development. Highly motivated students can use terminals to great advantage, but the sheer impersonality of the process is depressing to gregarious people.

Student bodies vary from campus to campus. In a highly selective college everyone is a very good student and comes from secondary school with the requisite knowledge and skills. Failure or mediocre performance can be a highly relative thing in those circumstances. If the criterion of accountability or assessment is achievement on standardized tests, e.g. the tests for admission to professional schools such as law and medicine, the outcome is pre-determined. Bright college students perform well on such tests, and the criterion may tell us more about the input of students into the college years than about what the college curriculum did for them. Much the same case can be made about the college whose feeder secondary schools yield ill-prepared students. There too, we may be assessing input variables rather than outcomes of the college experience. For most of American higher education, the reality catches both ends of the spectrum and faculties try to speed the best on their way while also broadening the horizons of the ill-prepared.

Today, faculties take such responsibilities seriously. They try to encourage the faint-hearted while resisting the decline of students. However, grade inflation over the last two decades has been the trend, as more and more students have attempted college curricula. Across the campus some departments have found themselves highly attractive to students. Courses in business schools present considerable competition for grades, and departments of anthropology have learned that vocationalism is currently triumphing over a detached, analytic view of the human animal and its condition. Engineering enrollments tend to be cyclic in all decades, and nursing schools are enrolling fewer students while that profession upgrades its standards from the Registered Nurse to the Bachelor of Science in Nursing. Assessment in these disciplines means different things; for business high enrollments mean greater selectivity, and for nursing performance on the State licensing examination is the obvious criterion for assessment of outcomes. It should be noted that the business graduates will be about 22 to 25 years of age, while nurses graduating from degree-completion programs might be, perhaps, ten years older. Obviously, the same yardstick of success may not serve such disparate groups fairly; one is at the beginning of a competitive career, and the other is well into a technical career of personal service.

There are variations across the disciplines which affect assessment of outcomes along the dimension of formal content to creativity. At one end are mathematics and, to a lesser extent, the natural sciences, in which content is formal, traditional and sequential. Students deal with received knowledge and learn to wrangle problems in a prescribed fashion. In contrast, there is studio art in which mastery of materials is complemented by skill at personal expression—a subjective matter for the most part. Students who are, respectively, comfortable and uncomfortable with authority find these two fields easy to work in. As a result, student satisfaction is high and the outcome of the college years satisfying.

Procedurally, there are correct solutions in the science-mathematics complex, although the distinction of applied and theoretical work relaxes the boundaries of method for imaginative students. The role of faculty as models for would-be scholars is determined by their own productivity, largely. Students will tolerate a good deal of ambiguity to hear a presentation by an eminent scholar. In the evaluation of college outcomes the opportunity to have had contact with such people, however brief, is highly prized. In turn, eminent scholars tend to see serious students as junior colleagues on the same road, but not quite as far along. This is especially the case with graduate students whose post-student career may be merely a shift of emphasis on the long road to eminence as a scholar.

In contrast, some fields emphasize the refinement of experience. Students in social work learn how social networks operate, but they must also learn to understand human relationships and to analyze the utterances of people in distress. The process presents a mirror to students who see themselves and their professors in light of the processes of human interaction. Assessment of outcomes in such a discipline suggests emphasis on satisfaction with one's grasp of the range of human problems and the inevitability of dilemmas. Content exists, and students learn the processes of social work, but it is insight and sensitivity, occasionally coupled with urgency, which characterizes effective graduates in social work.

Aspects of campus life which also affect student outcomes are some of the minor matters which, over several years, cumulate to a greater significance. For commuter campuses there is always the matter of parking. Campus police are helpful or hostile, and students reach their conclusions fairly quickly. Libraries with helpful staffs, business office clerks who keep a sense of proportion, and Registrar's procedures which are conciliatory leave lasting impressions. By these items we wish to convey that campus management which is sensitive to students as paying customers sets the stage for good outcomes. In an age of touchy consumers, irritated students complain, and go elsewhere if not treated fairly.

Finally, there is the undergraduate culture itself. On residential campuses it is based in shared experiences in dormitories and social groups. At Northeast Missouri State University, dormitory life is being upgraded into the form of residential colleges with an associated faculty for each. When left unstructured, the student network conveys fact and fiction, and is the major process of acculturation. Students learn to be students from other students. They learn that dormitory food must be bad because it is dormitory food, and that drinking a lot of beer is proof of maturity. Similarly, there are dress codes and styles which are chic and gauche. The student culture authoritatively states which professors are to be avoided, and which offices are helpful. Assessment of outcomes can view this aspect of the college years as important, or shun it in favor of recording academic achievement. Assessment for the purpose of general campus improvement should be sensitive to the student culture and use it to improve campus life. When the faculty are perceived as outside campus life because they are remote and inaccessible the initiative falls to the student culture. Contact with faculty early in students' careers is a way to ensure a healthy counterbalance to the myths which every campus culture transmits. Such contacts must be planned, since many students seem to go to great pains to resist advice and help from faculty and student personnel workers anxious to assist. Dropping-out of school can be the eventual outcome of a high degree of alienation, anomie and boredom even among well-prepared students.

The American College Student

Diverse institutions attract diverse student bodies. The major evidence of this axiom is the evolution of the undergraduate student body away from the common stereotype. It says that people who are academically well prepared go to college; they do so at eighteen and graduate four years later. The present undergraduate student body is quite different. Community and junior colleges take virtually anyone who can pay the fees; other institutions admit only the top five per cent from a national pool of talent and scholarships are readily available.

In the matter of age when attending college, the *Digest of Educational Statistics* (1986) reported the characteristics of college students up to age 34. The youngest were 14 years old, but the group between 30 and 34 years of age was 10.8 per cent. The group between 18 and 21 was 50.2 per cent of the total; when the 24-year-olds were included the proportion of 18 to 24-year-olds was 69.1 per cent. The significance is that almost one-third are outside the 18 to 24 year range.

In the same 1986 document it was reported that the sex ratio is almost identical and 49.2 per cent of college students aged 14 to 34 are females. The racial proportions of white and black are 85.4 per cent and 10.4 per cent; other groups account for 4.4 per cent. The most significant proportion is that one student in six or seven is black, a change from historical proportions. From the Digest we also learn that 51.8 per cent of college students are in the first and second years; 31.4 per cent are in their fourth or fifth years. The latter is important because fewer students enter college and leave exactly four years later. On urban commuter campuses, for example, a majority of undergraduates have jobs and take less than full loads, thereby stretching out the years to graduation. This has implications for assessment; it may be several years since students took a mathematics or science course as a part of general education, and so their achievement in such areas as graduating seniors may be low. Also, students who take years to graduate exhibit rather autonomous patterns of behavior and probably have quite unique expectations for the outcome of the college experience. The reason is probably greater maturity associated with being older and with experiences in the world of work.

In any consideration of outcomes we take into account where we start. American undergraduates tend to approach college admission in a fairly relaxed frame of mind. They experience anxiety over admission to a highly selective institution or an institution in an attractive climate, but they know there is a place for them somewhere. Their counterparts in the rest of the world tend to end the years of secondary education on a crescendo of demanding examinations for admission to college and competition for scarce places. In consequence, the achievement level of American college entrants varies from very good to abysmal. On the other hand, American students' ability to criticize and understand strikes some observers as superior. Research on the comparative performance of students in several countries has shown that mathematics scores are uniformly lower for American students. The same picture arises in other fields, but there have been improvements in key skills of students entering college. From the *Condition of Education*, a Federal document issued for 1986, it is apparent that English and mathematics test scores improved in the years 1972 to 1984. The proportion of high school students achieving scores of twenty-six or more as the English and mathematics sections of the ACT test (American College Testing Program) has risen significantly. The 1972 and 1984 proportions of high scores (≤ 26) were 0.7 per cent and 2.2 per cent for English. For mathematics achievement the percentages in the same years were 2.6 and 5.0. The proportion of high English scores tripled, and the proportion of high mathematics scores doubled. The relevance of this lies in the recognition that college entrants bring a base on which college builds. Most colleges offer elaborate programs designed to salvage students with weak skills and levels of preparation. These programs are often designed to compensate for twelve years of student indifference or, more rarely, lack of opportunity to learn. Today, colleges have a job of social salvage as a part of their mission. Accordingly, the value of such programs is a useful way to assess the outcomes of the campus' curriculum. We may expect that some students will graduate who would not have, otherwise.

However, it is not necessarily the case that students enroll in college in order to graduate. Some have more modest plans, and a few merely seek to postpone the end of adolescence and entry into the world of adult work. Here too we see autonomous plans and private goals, and achieving something less than a degree with very high grades may still be a source of personal satisfaction to students. In such cases they may speculate that graduating is not for them, a long-held suspicion contrary to family expectations, but a quite satisfying personal outcome. In that sense, which admittedly applies only to a few students, the assessment of outcomes by means of tests of achievement may miss the point entirely. In contrast, many older adults come to college with a hunger to learn which is quite uncompromised by vocational goals or advancement.

Black and White Colleges and Black Students

Campuses reflect the larger reality of society, and the reaction of young people to their college years summates their prior experiences. The study by Peterson *et al.* (1978) of black students on four predominantly white campuses showed that relations between the students and the campuses varied a good deal. The extent to which the campus chose to address the topic of race relations was the chief influence on the satisfaction and aspirations of black students. Fleming's (1984) research into the situation of black students used 3000 Freshmen and seniors in eight predominantly white and seven predominantly black colleges in four states. She concluded that black students make more progress towards maturity in black colleges. For black students to fare well on predominantly white campuses they need to find a 'supportive community'. That atmosphere, Fleming described as providing opportunities for friendships of all kinds, to participate in campus life, and to experience a sense of progress and success. From Allen's (1987) research the college experience of black students can be improved through:

Pre-collegiate programs of enrichment
Good coordination between secondary and higher education
Coaching to take standardized tests
Early admission and financial help
Orientation programs for freshmen
Acquisition of longitudinal data on student life
Coordination of existing campus services
Involvement of faculty
Presence of more blacks, especially females
Existence of value-added approach to campus life
Definite striving to increase numbers of black students

From the point of view of evaluation, the eleven points of Allen and the three of Fleming provide the basis for reviewing the scope and deciding the adequacy of efforts to assist minority students. The importance of that step cannot be overemphasized, for enrollments of black students are slipping. The problem is not just one of persuading high school seniors to attend college; it is preceded by the urban problem of trying to keep adolescents in school at all. For higher education, there is the problem of declining enrollments of black students in professional schools and in the graduate schools. Thomas (1987) examined black enrollment data in professional and graduate schools from the early 1980s and found minorities underrepresented, especially in the natural sciences and technical disciplines. In 1980/81, the two institutions awarding doctoral degrees in engineering were Cornell and Massachusetts-Amherst. Vigorous recruitment of prospective graduate students requires financial support; the Patricia Robert Harris Minority Graduate Fellowships of the United States government are an example of a relevant program which some campuses can draw on.

The American college student is far from the stereotype in personal characteristics and in motivation. We need to acknowledge the diversity of the non-traditional student body when formulating a plan to assess the outcomes of higher education. The outcomes envisaged need the ballast of who the students are, and where they personally have chosen to venture in their college experience. At the same time, consideration of outcomes needs to anticipate what the student body will be in years to come. In many respects it will resemble the national population as expressed in the local catchment area or in the hoped-for study body.

Evaluation of the college experience in a particular instance should be a configuration of common elements in which the local situation dictates the emphases. It should determine what is assessed, as well as the mode of assessment. At the level of the department, we emphasize the outcomes of a curriculum and seek ways to improve it. At the college level, there is the value of attending to shared outcomes of (for example) a program of general education, its machinery and costs in people and materials. At the campus level, the level of analysis and unit of measurement are more generic.

In their major review of the literature on program review, Conrad and Wilson (1985) list six purposes for which campuses have developed program reviews. They are:

1 To assess program quality, productivity, need and demand.
2 To improve the quality of academic offerings.
3 To ensure wise use of resources.
4 To determine the program's effectiveness and to consider possible modifications.
5 To facilitate academic planning and budgeting.
6 To satisfy state-level review requirements.

At the multi-campus or state-wide level evaluation resists specificity beyond costs and calling for reports from campuses. Ironically, the connection between policy making and specificity is probably negative, and those who have the least detailed knowledge may influence planning and budgeting the most. However, all groups subscribe to the belief that assessment at all levels should lead to formation of a better college experience for students. The challenge is to rise beyond summation of what prevails and to embark on improvements based on a detailed grasp of how things are at a given moment. Such improvements require transcending present facts and goals in order to frame a new vision for the college years.

In the last years of the twentieth century, the pattern of occupations is changing. Kutscher (1987) forecasted for the year 2000 a 'moderate' estimate of growth in service-producing jobs from 74,363,000 to 94,478,000. Agricultural jobs, in contrast, will drop from 3,252,000 to 2,917,000. Manufacturing jobs will decline from 18,994,000 to 18,160,000, and goods-producing jobs will shrink from 24,681,000 to 24,678,000, despite an overall increase in the population. Campus outcomes need to include preparation for life in the twenty-first century based on radical alternatives. There will be entirely new occupations and campuses need to prepare, as best they can foresee, to offer preparation not now available for narrow vocational opportunities. Of course, literacy and numeracy will continue to undergird all forms of college preparation, and those outcomes will persist. However, computer literacy at a high level may well be a necessary skill of college graduates; indeed, it may well be a routine outcome of secondary education.

Perspective

In summary, American higher education is a large, costly and diverse enterprise. The population it serves evolves, and in that respect resembles the condition of society on the threshold of the twenty-first century. To the patrons of universities, the campus can be a reassuring island of continuity in a sea of flux. That appreciation is correct in some respects, but it falls short of responsiveness to society's need for a population attuned to the challenges of the future and armed with the lessons of the past. Assessment of the university on a timely, periodic basis can be a way to preserve the best while preparing for new challenges and opportunities.

Chapter 2

Challenges

Accountability

In an era of increasing accountability organizations are frequently called upon to justify their activities. At the extreme, accountability takes the form of applying Occam's Razor to the need for agencies to exist. Higher education has faced less incisive trimming but has not been immune to the parsimonious trend in education which has closed elementary schools and, on occasion, had led to their sale for non-educational purposes. Within that frame of reference higher education has not fared badly, and only financial, but not instructional, failure of colleges has led to extinction.

On a more modest level, however, colleges have become inured to life in a steady state of reduced enrollments and finances, at best. Taking the place of expansionism have been budget reallocations, scrutiny of goals, and the search for avoidable duplication of programs which are accessible to the population. In recent years this process of review and accounting has posed the broad question of how much value has been added to the lives of young people by the experience of attending college. This version of auditing replaces the traditional faculty view that the outcomes of higher education are conceptual and so are also intangible. Replacing the self-serving position that no question is answerable is the call to answer questions of a particular nature. No longer is it enough to describe a college by describing its resources; now, we are pressed to document *outputs* rather than self-image. Output is a term whose manufacturing tenor is all too often expressed in naive but unavoidable terms. It is also expressed in the form of questions whose answers appear irrelevant or misleading, at times, to faculties. In the case of land–grant universities, service to the people of the state has structured evaluation to include assessment of the impact of the university on a broad clientele.

However, there is a core of significance in even a primitive empirical question. For higher education, it resides in the opportunity to demonstrate to the sceptical, to the credulous and also to the sophisticated that there are tangible outcomes to the undergraduate experience. Indeed, approached in a comprehensive fashion, the issue of the value added to human lives by college can become the basis for claiming support from the polity.

At the moment, however, the relationship requires that universities satisfy the public that there is value received for the substantial investment in higher education. Campuses are required to show that there is a tangible return in the form of demonstrable gains in the lives of college students upon graduation. In some contexts gain is defined as an increment on an achievement test. In others the sense of value added to the lives of young people is cast in the form of their evaluation of the gain. With this last approach gain is defined more generously, and the valuation arrived at is the product of the center of the complex, the student. Also, the range of items to be evaluated is broader and more flexible than achievement tests. The latter are difficult to construct and may not be sensitive to the personal aspirations which students bring to their curricular and campus experiences.

In the last analysis students are the best evaluators of the benefits of their experiences in college. However, the value they place upon the experience may not crystallize while they are in college, and may wax or wane as they evaluate their college days in the context of their post-collegiate years. In that formulation, the value added to people's lives will rise and fall as relevance to an immediate life situation rises and falls. Accordingly, college has multiple values rather than a single value, and so may need to be studied at different points in the post-collegiate years in order to assess it comprehensively. Such evaluation cannot depend on achievement tests since skills decay and testing becomes onerous to adults. However, evaluation which is more perceptive than substantive may be welcome to thoughtful people examining their lives from time to time.

Campus Models

The diversity of American higher education is striking. It ranges from extended secondary schooling for low-skilled students to high order elucidation of advanced knowledge for a social and intellectual élite. In between are all the variants of schooling and they are complicated by site — city or country campus, residential or commuter; by majority and minority status; by ideology — secular or religious; by sponsorship — public or private; and by scope — teaching or research emphasis. These few elements, at least, interact to create all combinations. Accordingly, the intent may be to prepare students for distinguished graduate schools or to keep semi-literate youth off the streets in the hope they may be eased through the years of susceptibility to delinquency or, in depressed areas, a lack of opportunity for employment. Another intent may be to take reasonably educated adolescents, give them time to mature or to begin to do so, and open their eyes to truth, beauty and the professors' ennobling view of the world. To parents this may mean something quite different as they hope for qualifications, economic independence and not too many unnerving ideas in their offspring. Accordingly, campus goals are blends of ideal and practical considerations and of the intended and accidental.

To the faculty who provide instruction the diversity of higher education models is enormous, leading Turnbull (1985) to report that professors fear that evaluations of higher education are likely to be simplistic, incomplete and insensitive to differences in campus' missions. One response of campus leaders is to press for clarity of mission (Christ-Janer, 1980) and to seek new tools for campus management (Perlman, 1979). Occasionally, a campus President has taken the initiative and led the campus to great public acceptance (*In Pursuit . . .*, 1984), as at Northeast Missouri State University under Dr Charles McClain (Gilley, Fulmer and Reithlingshofer, 1986; McClain and Krueger, 1985; Ewell, 1987).

Assessment

When learners are young, exploration of their achievements is fairly straightforward. We can specify content, for example, corpus of words to be read, understood and applied, or a simple manipulation of a set of numbers by subtraction. With college students we have progressed to understandings of a high order and the expectation that they will be capable of generating information as active and creative scholars. At that high level of cognitive operations assessment is not easy since there is a high ceiling to student performance and someone—the examiner or test constructor—has to be at or above the students' ceiling level. In general, test constructors have managed to perform well and we have tests with high ceilings of attainment. It is noteworthy that a student achieved a perfect score in 1986 on a national college entrance test, however.

At the moment there is no shortage of tests of aptitude but tests of achievement are not so readily available. The ACT College Outcomes Measures Program (COMP), which we will describe in chapter 5, is an example of achievement tests. In recent years there has been a spurt in attention to writing competence. The topic has resisted incorporation into formats permitting easy and quick scoring since there are problems of reliability and objectivity. Assessment of writing is a time-consuming, subjective process and procedures require several readers who consciously use uniform procedures.

Finally, there is the question of who is to take such tests. If the college experience is to be assessed we need to test people before and after. For residential campuses this is fairly straightforward. However, many students today transfer, drop out — and back in — and may spend six rather than four years earning a degree. In the case of exit tests, the time-point may reveal the status of current graduates. But people continue to grow and mature; as a result assessment at graduation may be premature. On the other hand, use of the achievement measures with people some years out of college, a necessary continuity, may be hard to effect. In addition we can only anticipate decline in achievement test scores after college, and in proportion to the years since graduation. On that basis, appraisal of new and mature graduates may require use of criterion measures not vulnerable to early decay of achievement and not threatening, or time-consuming, to people out of college for several years.

Accountability

Historically, the matter of accountability has been handled by descriptions of input variables — qualifications of faculty, the size of the library and traits of students. Reputation of a high order has been a self-sustained process in which being called reputable led to affirmation by other institutions. This has especially been the case in graduate studies where repute has traditionally been the measure cultivated. Its negative effects can be seen currently in attacks on the peer review system of review for contracts and grants. Critics charge that campuses of high repute favor applications from other campuses of high repute, to the detriment of competent proposals from less well-known campuses. In that sense, the current call to assess the value of the college experience is entirely appropriate for it may be that the emperor is really without new clothes and really looks like other academic types. There is a strain of populism in such themes which tends to escape attention.

To William J. Bennett in 1984 the call to evaluate was a cry to return to a lost heritage, the legacy of the humanities scarcely considered by vocationally intent students. On the other hand, Lynne V. Cheney's (1988) report on the conditions of the humanities in America (Text, 1988) was more sanguine. On the premise that a humane education can occur off-campus, it was apparent to Cheney that popular culture and the several media were presenting books, plays, music and art to a quite large audience. To be sure, there was erosion at some points, according to the report, but there were gains for the humanities in several areas of living.

A clear call came from the nation's governors in 1986. In the document, *Time for Results*, (Alexander, Clinton and Keene, 1986) the Honorable John Ashcroft of Missouri stated,

> The public has a right to know what it is getting for its expenditure of tax resources; the public has a right to know and understand the quality of undergraduate education that young people receive from publicly funded colleges and universities. They have a right to know that their resources are being wisely invested and committed.

In Missouri, the governor, the Honorable John Ashcroft, called attention to another element of the past, now foregone, the length of the instructional year. It is reported (Ashcroft, 1987) that the instructional year has shrunk by an average of eleven days in the last forty years. Over four years that amounts to forty-four instructional days or nine weeks of five days. Governor Ashcroft noted that this decline was a national trend, finding it, 'hardly surprising — to note that a graph of Missouri's shortening academic years conspicuously resembles graphs of deteriorating nation-wide performance on many standardized tests'. The view of Bennett and of the governors is a request to learn more about the process variables of higher education and the outcomes. Of the two sets of variables, process and outcomes, greater attention is paid, currently, to outcomes. We now turn to some observations on how to assess the college experience.

When the question of what the students get out of school is examined, interesting results emerge. Powell's (1985) study found three outcomes in former students' autobiographies of their school years. They were formation of values and attitudes, cognitive development and identification of elements which helped and hindered learning. In the research by Marion and Cheek (1985) it turned out that retrospection was mediated by current success or failure. In 1985 Kuh summarized several major studies of the impact of going to college and concluded that the lives of people attending college were improved in many ways. Baktari and Grasso's (1985) research, however, showed that economic gains from attending college are not always very high, initially.

A different approach has been introduced by Robert Pace (1983) who believed that there are broad sets of outcomes which most students can examine and rate for adequacy. In his *College Student Experiences* questionnaire of eight pages Pace includes twenty-one items of possible gain. What is relevant to our discussion of student models is that Pace's criteria of gain are broader than any single campus or curriculum (see table 6), recalling that students enroll in colleges which may be large or small, secular or religious, private or public, etc. It is important to note that Pace's twenty-one items deal with potential outcomes, relevant and irrelevant. This approach may be contrasted with specifying content of the curriculum and deducing success or failure at the bar of accountability by exploring achievement in the content. By implication, the specificity of content points to standardized tests of achievement. That is a sensible approach as far as it goes, but it tends to slight several other propositions. One of them is that in some fields there is little or no consensus about common undergraduate content, for example, biology. A second is that baseline data for entering students may be the peak. When a second test is given four years later there may have been predictable decay of knowledge, for example, in algebra, because students took one course as Freshmen. These points are not absolute barriers to content testing, but indicate that the approach, like all others, is not beyond criticism.

For some students entrance examinations for professional schools such as medicine, law and business are suitable criteria. The ultimate test of the student model is, as Astin (1977) pointed out, the achievement of those who went to college versus those who did not. However, as Bennett (Adelman, 1986) has observed, half of all high school graduates go on to college. He points out that test scores on eleven of fifteen content tests of the Graduate Record Examination declined between 1964 and 1982. In that same period we achieved the 50 per cent continuation rate, so that the traditional achievers were joined by students of lesser ability and attainment. One fact is the reciprocal of the other.

Student Models

To some people, students at all ages are so many empty cups to be filled from a large container. The process is one-way and someone in authority specifies the content to be poured into passive learners. To others, learners are to be turned into reflective people by absorbing great ideas of the past. Still another of the many variants is that learners are in college to explore as broadly as possible their cultural and intellectual inheritance. Slightly different are the church formulations of learners as essentially spiritual creatures to be guided to personal growth and occupational competence in which ethical and religious precepts will prevail.

A different kind of model adopts a formulation of the college years as a rite of passage in which people move from one Eriksonian (Erikson, 1968) stage or Piagetian level (Piaget, 1972) to the next. In the Alverno College formulation (Mentkowski and Loacker, 1985; Loacker, Cromwell and O'Brien, 1986) the model specifies that the student acquires information about personal progress and uses it to improve personal achievement. Knowing how much has been learned is used internally by the student, while the same information can be used by the college to fine-tune teaching and the curriculum.

Student Variables

The Alverno model postulates a learner for whom nothing has a higher priority than attainment of learning. However, as there are campuses which do not resemble Alverno with its small, relatively personalized style, so there are other kinds of students. Some are part-time at their studies, and such students have a less enriched perception of campus life (Carnegie, 1986). Mature students may need to earn a living to support dependents as their highest priority. Other students are mature rather than in the age 18 to 22 stereotype and choose to study for their own, autonomous reasons rather than those espoused by campus committees. Some students are motivated and others are not. From Komarovsky's (1985) research it is clear that dynamic changes occurred within students at a women's college. They moved from separation anxieties as freshmen to fairly clear vocational choice as seniors. The socialization process, apart from the curriculum, matured the young women. Across the whole range of human traits are examples of dispositions which exist on campus and coincide with the model of student aptitudes and ambitions to various degrees. In that respect the possibilities for misunderstandings and discrepancies are probably higher now than ever before. The current generation of students is conservative and appears to be quite vocational and materialistic in outlook. As a result, enrollments are up in business schools and down in liberal arts fields. Faculty may have one formulation of curricular objectives while students in attendance may have another; faculty may wish to open windows for students they consider parochial, while students may aspire to a good job in wholly trade school terms. University planners may see the college years as the first stage in life-long learning. In contrast, some students aspire to no more than sampling an attractive mode of life after high school for a semester or two.

The State

In any case the complex of questions about goals and outcomes has moved off the campus into the public forum. Government in Missouri, Georgia, Florida, Tennesse, South Dakota, New Jersey and other states has moved to establish a state role in the appraisal of education for undergraduates (Hartle, 1986; Rentz, 1979; Southern. . . 1985; Stevens and Hamlett, 1983). In Skinner and Tafel's (1986) report on Ohio there is a broad range of criteria indicating acceptance of the proposition that more than one output measure may be relevant. The idiom of outputs implies inputs, and we may reasonably consider what the inputs, in the form of financial support, across the fifty states have been. Of course, the topic applies only to public higher education, although the majority of institutions of higher education are public, and state support is complemented by fees and other income. However, those last two sources are add–ons to the support authorized by legislators and governors. In table 4 we present data for 1986/87 on the scope of interest in higher education, the subvention and costs to students. There, we see that states vary considerably in the proportion of students who go on to college. In the District of Columbia only 12.5 persons per 1000 of the population attend college; of course, Washington has a high proportion of Federal employees and many adults have college degrees; on the other hand, the District has many poor people, so that the rate of 12.5 is credible. To that we add that the District of Columbia has not had a tradition of public higher education, and its University is a recent innovation, although the adjoining states have major institutions close by; for example, the University of Maryland at College Park. At the opposite extreme is North Dakota, 44.3 per 1000 of whose small population are enrolled annually.

Table 4: States' revenues applied to public higher education 1986 (excludes US service schools)

State	State allocation (000)	Enrollment	Per capita allocation (000)
	28,071,070	9,726,168	2.88
Alabama	624,942	160,437	3.89
Alaska	153,321	26,359	5.81
Arizona	417,244	213,566	1.95
Arkansas	256,238	68,760	3.72
California	4,150,576	1,526,039	2.72
Colorado	354,604	157,521	2.25
Connecticut	259,600	98,828	2.62

Table 4. (continued).

State	State allocation (000)	Enrollment	Per capita allocation (000)
Delaware	85,832	28,894	2.97
District of Columbia	0	11,800	—
Florida	1,070,305	385,436	2.77
Georgia	641,490	147,269	4.35
Hawaii	192,094	42,593	4.51
Idaho	115,659	35,532	3.25
Illinois	1,081,259	530,539	2.04
Indiana	611,657	194,134	3.15
Iowa	400,286	110,439	3.62
Kansas	344,042	129,839	2.65
Kentucky	450,831	115,057	3.92
Louisiana	532,174	146,297	3.64
Maine	99,450	34,460	2.88
Maryland	492,948	199,433	2.47
Massachusetts	534,002	178,612	2.99
Michigan	1,053,665	445,760	2.31
Minnesota	509,999	178,790	2.85
Mississippi	330,527	89,925	3.67
Missouri	448,760	168,883	2.66
Montana	91,805	30,645	2.99
Nebraska	209,620	84,262	2.48
Nevada	95,412	46,490	2.05
New Hampshire	48,958	28,732	1.70
New Jersey	662,898	235,773	2.81
New Mexico	190,781	78,565	2.43
New York	2,026,746	573,452	3.53
North Carolina	989,528	262,639	3.77
North Dakota	115,679	34,898	3.31
Ohio	1,019,197	384,787	2.65
Oklahoma	409,613	149,043	2.75
Oregon	290,669	125,877	2.31
Pennsylvania	735,151	304,190	2.41
Rhode Island	101,776	35,509	2.86
South Carolina	470,757	108,191	4.35
South Dakota	63,037	24,036	2.62
Tennessee	498,786	149,445	3.33
Texas	2,266,662	685,544	3.30
Utah	248,250	73,072	3.40
Vermont	32,094	18,734	1.71
Virginia	738,865	265,687	2.78
Washington	588,665	212,332	2.77
West Virginia	212,551	67,078	3.17
Wisconsin	638,978	244,948	2.61
Wyoming	113,087	23,735	4.76

Source: Adapted from, *Digest of Educational Statistics 1988,* Washington, DC, US Department of Education, 1988.

Reciprocally, cost to the student is highest in Vermont where the net tuition is $4622. It is lowest in California where the typical student paid $497, or one-tenth, approximately, of the fees in Vermont. In the middle, at approximately $1200, are college students in Oregon, Kentucky and South Dakota.

Consideration of the data in table 4 allows us to formulate a major observation for the public forum; namely, that output can be reasonably expected to relate to input. Given the high allocation of State funds to colleges the call to accountability is quite reasonable. But does the same call ring as true in states such as Vermont where comparatively little of the colleges' budget comes from the State treasury? Theoretically, one might argue that modest State effort leads to proportionately higher student fees and so to a proportionately reduced State claim for accountability; by implication, individual fee payers have the stronger claim to accountability in such cases.

In general, a review of assessment of outcomes of higher education has much the same result as close examination of other public issues. That is, there are core questions of validity, investment and relevance. These topics are transmogrified by debate into a complex of issues with varying degrees of salience for different participants. Specification of criteria and evidence unfolds into an array of choices because there are many levels of investments and kinds of college, students and objectives. At the same time, the range of ways to assess the outcomes of higher education also expands. The result is a matrix of students, campuses, goals and modes of assessment. To the research worker, the challenge is to select the salient and optimal array from the range of combinations.

Outcomes

A topic of no small importance is the specification of what college graduates can do which they could not do after completing secondary education. The specifics in question describe the impact of the college experience. In theory, the question should be answered by assessing college graduates and also assessing people who did not attend college — but possessing identical traits of achievement, aptitude and motivation. Both groups should be tested on the same day at the time one group completes the college experience. Of course, such evaluation is not possible; in reality, we cannot create true experiments in which we randomly assign one student to college and another to something else. It follows that the assessment of outcomes is rarely a true experiment, but is usually a quasi-experiment; that is, it is a serious enquiry into phenomena at hand and not usually under the investigator's total control.

A useful step is to specify outcomes in functional terms. One category is content; that is, a student of mathematics should know how to execute specific mathematical tasks such as solving differential equations. In some fields there has long been consensus in this matter. PhD curricula in physics are fairly homogeneous, and health disciplines tend to provide uniform content in order to prepare students for licensing examinations. In other fields, of which history is an example, there is no such uniformity and students give an additional, personal flavor to their courses once a fairly small core requirement has been met. We conclude that course content is a fairly straightforward matter in some fields but not in others.

On the other hand, there are skills which apply in all fields. Reading at a high level of comprehension in a given field seems a skill shared by all. Analysis of problems, however, depends on which field we are considering. Problem solving is a mode for civil engineering students which requires much applied activity. For philosophy majors it may range from armchair speculation to mastery of the complexity of syllogisms. Writing effectively is still another skill which all fields share. For law students the desired level is prose devoid of ornamentation; for students of creative writing and poetry effective writing takes a quite different form. Use of skills as a component of outcomes is an important and useful element. A major aspect of skills is the technical difficulty of devising tasks to measure them. Outcome measures of skills must be scoreable and they must tap vital operations. At one time, American colleges required comprehensive final examinatons to qualify for degrees. The possibility of such a requirement returning to American higher education exists, as some State governments require all seniors to be tested, and the data reported. Comparisons across institutions with differing entrance requirements and differing missions would not deter oversimplified conclusions and prescriptions.

In many parts of the world this is still the case, and a final, summatory examination covers the entire curriculum. In such programs semester examinations are irrelevant, and attendance at classes is less critical. On the other hand, the American pattern of semester examinations sets the stage for defining knowledge and skills by levels at narrow intervals. That possibility can be viewed as competency testing in a sequence of qualifying experiences. It is especially relevant in mathematics, for example, where content and skills are quite sequential, but less so in the fields where personal creativity and expression are the desired outcomes. In the latter instance, the entire question is subjective and aesthetic, and poses enormous challenges to objectivity—which may in fact, be irrelevant.

In theory, it is possible to assess both skills and content at the same time. Such sophistication is implicit and makes test construction difficult and slow.

Goals

Assessment in higher education is a process by which we hope to learn that colleges are doing successfully what they have proposed to do. The process requires that colleges have a clear set of goals so that the assessment process can be a focused enquiry. The specification of goals of education is an endless territory. At the State University of New York at Albany the purposes of the University were set forth as the discovery, transmittal and application of knowledge on behalf of society. The functions are interrelated, of course, and they are accomplished through the activities of teaching, research and consultation. In greater detail, SUNY-Albany's goals fall into two groups. There are eight goals for *student* development.

  (i)   To develop skills of critical thinking and reasoning.
 (ii)   To develop and foster the process of intellectual discovery and explanation of the unknown.
(iii)   To develop an awareness and interest in the breadth of human intellectual achievement and cultural experience.
 (iv)   To facilitate emotional development and clarification of personal values.
  (v)   To facilitate social development and effectiveness in interpersonal relationships.
 (vi)   To facilitate physical development, health, and well-being.
(vii)   To prepare students for personally satisfying careers.
(viii)   To maintain a campus environment which will foster a sense of community and social responsibility.

In addition, there are three goals for *societal* development:

  (i)   To contribute to the general advancement of knowledge and to the solution of societal problems.
 (ii)   To offer opportunities for life-long learning as an integral part of institutional activities.
(iii)   To contribute to the development of the local area through the provision of cultural and clinical services which reinforce educational mission. (Mission Review, 1981)

These eleven goals in two domains are institution-wide, and set the stage for each academic unit to develop more specific and appropriate objectives.

The Alverno College faculty have defined eight abilities as developmental, holistic and transferable, toward which they orient their teaching (Alverno College Faculty, 1985, third edition). The eight outcomes of an integrated liberal arts and professional education at Alverno are effectiveness in:

Communication
Analysis
Problem solving
Valuing
Social interaction
Taking responsibility for the global environment
Responsible citizenship
Aesthetic responsiveness

Further, faculty assess for these abilities across the curriculum and credential them for graduation (Alverno College Faculty, 1979 rev. 1985; Loacker, Cromwell and O'Brien, 1986). The college conducts research and evaluation to establish the validity of these abilities for later personal growth and professional performance (Mentkowski and Loacker, 1985; Mentkowski, 1988).

At an unnamed large southern university Marion and Cheek (1985) reported alumni perceptions of success, due to college, in growth in the following eight target areas or goals:

Preparation for further graduate or professional education
Development or improvement of employment skills
Enhanced reasoning ability
Learning to communicate effectively
Developing an appreciation of the arts
Developing an awareness of other cultures and philosophies
Reaching a better understanding of one's self
Increased skill at human relations

A similar study reported by Kuh (1985) summarized a number of original studies on outcomes in the areas of:

Acquisition of knowledge
Intellectual development
Social development
Personal development
Career and vocational development

In 1985, the Association of American Colleges issued a report on the college curriculum (*Integrity*. . . . 1985) and offered a set of 'essential experiences' for undergraduates. The Association recommended that undergraduates undergo nine essential experiences within the curriculum. They are:

Enquiry, abstract logical thinking, critical analysis
Literacy: writing, reading, speaking, listening
Understanding numerical data
Historical consciousness
Science
Values
Art
International and multicultural experiences
Study in depth

Benderson (1986) has called attention to the value of providing nine areas of instruction which may be summarized as:

Critical thinking	Values
Literacy and communication	Art
Understanding numbers	Cross-cultural experiences
Sense of history	Study in depth
Science	

Northeast Missouri State University (Ewell, 1987a) set forth three main goals, with focused questions under each of the three, for the next five years, as follows:

To graduate students at the baccalaureate level possessing considerable breadth of liberal learning.

To graduate students who are nationally competitive in their major fields, and who demonstrate mastery of their discipline's subject matter and proficiency with its distractive methods of enquiry.

To graduate students who possess self-esteem, self-confidence, and readiness to accept the challenges of adult life, sufficient to meet the requirements of change and professional/career adaptation, and to contribute constructively and creatively to society.

At the University of Missouri–St Louis, in 1987, the faculty defined the goal of undergraduate education to be a process which will: foster sound judgment, clarity of expression in writing, aesthetic refinement, and sharpened analytical skills through its undergraduate general education curriculum. All students complete courses in the social and natural sciences and the humanities as well as in writing and mathematics. Students also receive specialized education while pursuing a baccalaureate degree in a specific academic discipline.

University of Missouri-St Louis faculty develop students' reading, speaking, writing and cognitive skills by improving their ability to investigate, analyze and solve problems. Some courses fulfilling the general education requirements expand students' knowledge of group interaction through the study of psychology, political science and economics. Other courses increase students' understanding of the role and effects of science and technology in modern life. Cultural and civic awareness is fostered through the study of history and contemporary society of the United States as well as other cultures, both Western and non-Western, as reflected in language, music, literature, philosophy, religion, history and art.

Through this curriculum, University of Missouri-St Louis faculty promote the development of each student as a person who enjoys and is committed to learning for life as well as providing basic preparation and background for further education and specialization for a career in a professional, academic, or scientific field.

These eight statements of outcomes, established prospectively or retrospectively, and in terse outline form or as prose, provide criteria for assessment. Whatever the choices are, and they tend to be similar by domains, they require translation from rhetorical to operational terms. That is, the process of assessment requires exact statements so that hypotheses can be formulated for empirical, i.e. data-specific, studies. This process is inevitable, since goal statements are designed to communicate with a wide range of people and so require a degree of latitude in phrasing. For example, no one specifies target rates of reading and comprehension of several types of text, from novels to chemistry tests, as goals of undergraduate education; nor do they state target scores or percentages of passing on State licensing examinations in law and the health sciences. Yet, at the point of assessment, a high degree of clarity is essential.

One implication of the emphasis on empirically generated data on outcomes is the comparability of campuses which use similar criterion measures. Within a state's system of colleges or an accrediting body's region it would be possible to make comparisons. Of course, such comparisons should be modulated by recognizing different missions. This last point is probably too fine for the general public to appreciate; and it might well get lost in a legislative debate on getting value for the investment of public funds. There is a folk observation attributed to the eponymous Murphy which says that if something could happen it will, eventually, happen. The middle 'worst case' is that public bodies would require uniform data, and the worst 'worst case' is that they would require minimal levels of individual achievement for graduation. The former seems distasteful but not improbable, and the latter would precipitate a major response from colleges.

In general, the empiricism of the times has been hard on the relaxed language of mission statements and the reference to campus goals in college bulletins. The idiom of rhetoric, which set forth lofty ambitions in inspiring language, has been replaced by the idiom of measurement. The result is that we need language which encourages translation into terms amenable to measurement. Conversely, it is possible, but unwise, to take measuring instruments and define the goals in terms of what can be measured.

In some respects, the matter is predetermined by the locus of authority. For some people, e.g. Loacker, Cromwell and O'Brien (1986) the emphasis is a humanistic concern for the growth of individuals. From that point of view, empirical evaluation is modulated by attention to individual learners. Rather different is the perspective of those who see the college experience more remotely. For some of them, the evaluation idiom covers everything from human learning to the performance of battleships. The term, 'performance indicators' may be used to bring to bear on students' learning econometric idioms and cost/benefit ratios. Such an approach may be methodologically driven when several institutions must be evaluated, and the metric is not so much individual learners as aggregates in the thousands. A sympathetic use of performance indicators may be seen in the list of fourteen items, and their characteristics, in the work of Cave, Hanney, Kogan and Trevett (1988). They speak of performance indicators as devices which can be used developmentally rather than punitively in the assessment of components of complex systems. We may expect to see performance indicators become more subtle, and their analysis less of a bludgeon, in time.

However, it is prudent to keep in mind that there are some institutions whose goals do not permit simple assessment. For a naval academy the ultimate criterion is battles lost and won; for a school founded for religious purposes the ultimate criterion may be the salvation of souls. The challenge is to operationally define goals, while not falling into the methodological trap of concluding that only the empirically measurable is worth pursuing.

Chapter 3

Assessment

To engage in assessment of student outcomes is sensible, because it tells us if the customers thought the experience profitable. We now turn to evaluation of the processes which led to the student outcomes — the programs and the faculties who operate them. It should be pointed out, to begin with, that the relationship between means and outputs is approximate. The relationship could not really be otherwise since the means and the realization of the ends are mediated by the complexities of college-age learners. As we saw earlier, they are no longer the familiar homogeneous cluster of white middle class people. They are wider in age, more diverse in economic and ethnic origins, and quite capable of imposing their own value systems on whatever experience they are brought to. In that respect they treat higher education and its received values much as they treat religion and department stores; they choose selectively from what is offered, absorb it on their own terms and reject the more high flown verbiage. In short, they operate in relation to ideas as they operate in the cafeteria. They pick and choose, select and reject. Bloom (1987) pointed out that students are incredulous when they encounter non-relative values. Lest this seem too nihilistic it is the quality which makes Americans bad Montessori-ites and worse Marxists.

These remarks do not obviate the need to assess the means chosen to produce student outcomes, the academic units and their programs. Rather, the effect is to modulate the relationship between means and outcomes. The academic units cannot take excessive credit for student accomplishments, for they are partners at best, rather than masters, of that lively creature, the college student.

A campus plan for assessment is no small undertaking. As with all plans which are campus-wide, the support of major constituencies is vital. On some campuses the process of assessment is continuous and one cycle of review is followed by another. The process is paralleled by the cycles of external review as professional associations and accrediting bodies make their assessments, so that a given academic unit may be subject to two reviews in the same year or in adjacent years. In that situation, the campus goal might be to emphasize the external review and conduct the internal review of a program and of student outcomes as a supplementary activity.

A major choice for campus level assessment is whether to review non-academic elements on campus. Presumably, they exist in order to pursue the campus mission, and units such as student affairs influence student life considerably. On residential campuses they house and feed students and minister to the crises of young lives. More remote are the business offices and building maintenance services. Scrutiny of them may not be central to the instructional mission, but may be justified by the observation that everyone benefits from an appraisal.

For schools, departments and institutes the objectives of assessment are broad. At one extreme is the question of continuation. Research institutes established to face a problem in one decade are not necessarily relevant in the next decade. An example is a research institute founded in the years when space research was a major emphasis. Today, there may be a more pressing need to invest in a more current form of campus-industry liaison; review on a scheduled basis can help decide which units have outlived their original purpose. The decision may be aided by considering the proportion of the budget drawn from campus-versus-external sources. In the case of departments and professional schools, evaluation has objectives beyond relevance and fiscal effectiveness; these include assessment of the curriculum, trends in enrollment — some programs experiencing declines while others expand — and the effectiveness of graduates. The latter is an entire complex involving the satisfactions of students, employers and past graduates. In addition, the research productivity of the faculty, attraction of funds and the rate of tenuring recently hired faculty are important.

In theory, all levels and sectors reviewed can contribute to campus planning. However, budgets may be planned two years ahead, and it is not easy to incorporate assessment data fully into campus planning. Budgets are people-intensive, and tenure reduces flexibility, except in the very lowest ranks where annual or semester appointments are more likely.

Self-Study

From the campus point of view, the major tool of academic assessment is self-study of a unit. It is supplemented by the view of people who are drawn from the other departments and, occasionally, from other campuses. When self-studies are used on campus they require formal, specified detail for a unit to follow. An advantage of this approach is that all units are treated similarly, recognizing the value of occasional deviations reflecting particular circumstances. We now present examples of topics which self-studies might employ.

Mission and Goals Statement

It is vital that each campus unit provide a formal statement of mission, a brief statement in which the reason for a unit existing is set forth. Such a statement may be elaborated by development of particular goals, especially when an academic unit has broad responsibilities. In such statements we can identify production of specific graduates. We also recognize that some academic units exist primarily to provide general education, and generate only a few graduates. For example, on many campuses anthropology provides interesting courses for the liberal education of students, but not many people major in anthropology, at the moment. In contrast, the mission of (for example) a School of Mortuary Science would be wholly to produce undertakers.

Program Data

A unit can learn much about itself by the process of counting the number of students, student credit hours, enrollments per course and the number of sections per course. Usually, such data are assembled for a given year, and trend data in the form of previous and projected enrollments are developed. In units with a heavy service load to general education or to other departments, for example, economics providing courses for business majors, the level of courses is a vital piece of information. It usually turns out that much of the instructional load is underclassmen, and there may be few junior or senior year courses. When that is the case, and there is no graduate program, the cost of instruction per credit hour remains high. PhD programs can provide lecturers and other non-tenure track positions for Freshmen and Sophomore courses; in that case the cost of instruction is low, and that component of instruction may justify small enrollment senior courses for majors taught by full professors. Only explicit program data can set forth the fiscal structure of an academic program. In curricular terms, an academic unit may present data on good teaching; only detailed information can provide an explanation of the costs associated with instruction. In fiscal terms we may have the paradox of expensive graduate programs providing inexpensive undergraduate instructors which, in turn, helps justify the expensive graduate program.

Faculty, Staff and Students

The preceding matter brings us to a more focused consideration of personnel. To continue with faculty, we need to know how many there are by head count, full-time equivalent (FTE), in order to account for part-time instructors and by rank. It is also important to know the age, sex and ethnic composition of a faculty since pursuit of affirmative action goals may require a clear picture of underrepresented groups. Age is important since many faculties are almost completely tenured, and projections for vacancies by retirement are useful for planning revitalization of faculties by recruitment. However, the picture of retirement as a device for projecting faculty vacancies is clouded since mandatory ages for retiring are less forceful than in the past. At the same time some campuses now have voluntary programs of early retirement, and age data can be useful information for planning. Much the same statement can be made about staff. Another item of value is a set of up-to-date curriculum vitae for all faculty. Efficiency requires that numerical information be recorded in computer-based data banks for ease of retrieval and for updating.

In the case of students it is essential that departments know who their clients are. On residential campuses, programs reflect the full-time status of students, although there are part-timers. On commuter campuses there may be many working students whose schedules may not permit a pattern of courses suitable for residential students. Such people tend to take extra years to graduate, so that course offerings meeting the reality of their needs are cycled over ten or more semesters. Another example of useful data is knowing the aptitudes of students entering programs. For programs centered in the junior year, the press of numbers may require high selectivity. Business schools, for example, may be free to require an above average grade point average plus total completion of all general education requirements at the time of application. Less popular fields can be more accommodating. Data on student characteristics can frame sensible, workable policies. Data on student achievement at the time of graduation is increasingly important. Some State governments and Board of Trustees require test data on the achievement of graduating Seniors. Such tests exist in some fields and require construction in others.

Grades are a traditional way to measure outcomes, but grading standards vary from field to field across campus. On the other hand, year-by-year data on grades when plotted against aptitude measures can help a department decide if its grading standards have remained stable.

Staff Views

From the point of view of assessing the views of the campus community we tend to slight the views of non-academic staff. Their ranks include people whose experience with unit administrators, faculty, staff and students has led to useful if informal perceptions. Personnel office specialists know which administrators cannot retain secretaries. Computer centre administrators know whose students are well prepared. Research office personnel know which departments are at least trying to pursue funds. Graduate school specialists know which students receive good and bad advice as they struggle towards degrees. Library staff usually know the faculty who work there a good deal, who use interlibrary loan to access scarce materials, and who order the latest books.

Service Activities

The American university tends to pride itself on being a good neighbor in the community. An expression of that at the national level was the Morrill Act of 1862 which funded higher education on the basis of a service component. Historically, the concept has been expressed through service to agriculture, a concept which history and the nature of society have rendered partially obsolete. Administrators of extension services have been slow to apply their Federal pass-through funds into urban areas in recent years. For urban campuses, evaluation of service activities is quite important; the typical campus uses metropolitan facilities as a field resource for recruiting students and training them. Urban agencies call on campus faculties to provide consultation, give talks, and conduct research. These are healthy, reciprocal relationships in which both town and gown benefit. An appraisal of such activities is more appropriate for professional schools and applied fields. For more rarified disciplines expectations can be modest. Specialists in ancient history should not be expected to become members of Rotary and other linkage groups, and their time is better invested in the library.

Facilities

A vital topic in evaluation is the nature and extent of facilities. Description in the form of offices and people per office, or square yard of floor space, is a highly useful piece of information. Similarly, laboratories and the availability of specialized space such as clean rooms and ventilated areas is critical information. Storage space, and the presence of space for animals and radioactive materials needs to be appraised. In the last two examples there are quality considerations as well as Federal standards which must be complied with. Evaluation of such space and the procedures for its management are vital elements in assessment of academic units and of non-academic, support services.

All units share some campus-wide facilities. Computing is an example of a resource whose relevance to an academic unit varies as the technology evolves. Today, computing is used in a mixed mode; that is, some work requires access to a large, usually centralized unit, while many jobs can be performed on local equipment the size of a typewriter. In this regard, the funding model shared by units for computing, is a kind of facility. The range of models is broad, from a 'free good', i.e. unlimited access, to a system of recovery of centrally assigned funds considered to be real, 'hard' dollars. By implication, exhausting one's balance of such resources ends access to data processing until the user's account is replenished by central funds or department resources.

Budget

Few things are as central to evaluation as a grasp of budget detail. Campuses are personnel-intensive and most funds are tied-up in commitments of at least annual length to instructors. In the case of tenured faculty the obligations are complex. On closer examination, the departments on campus vary in their expenditures for equipment. This component of budget is large in the sciences and in some professional schools. Further, equipment needs to be replaced, and the decision is often dictated by marketing strategies of vendors who raise maintenance costs for equipment made obsolete by their introduction of new models.

A useful picture of the salary and benefits portions of budgets presents data by rank and years of service. Where faculty are on salary schedules the situation may be clear but inflexible. In the case of salary systems based on merit and market considerations, data can reveal the range of salaries. Also helpful is the picture of salaries for junior people such as teaching assistants and part-time, call staff. When budget data across departments is arrayed the range is considerable. This is natural since disciplines vary in their need for faculty; professors of surgery or accounting are hard to attract and to keep without competitive salaries.

A vital component of budgets is the portion consisting of external funds. Such monies are attracted by research contracts and gifts; the latter are infrequent but may be spectacular. In the case of research funds they are available in engineering, the sciences and health professions, and virtually unknown in the humanities. Accordingly, evaluation of the soft portion of academic budgets presumes an informed grasp of the academic enterprise and of the funding possibilities field by field. In some respects the proportion of the budget composed of research funds can be an index of the intellectual life of a faculty. In the case of PhD granting programs the presence of soft research money is a device to support graduate students. A budgetary analysis, accordingly, can also be a quality analysis.

One of the exercises in budgetary analyses is the calculation of ratios. For example, it can be useful to generate comparative data on research dollars raised per faculty member, or for non-salary dollars per faculty member. Any two numbers can yield a ratio, however, and we must specify with care and reason any ratios we use to evaluate budgets and units. It makes sense to calculate ratios which relate salary costs to student credit hours since the ratio describes costs per unit of instruction, setting apart equipment for the moment. On the other hand, calculating the ratio of class size to salary totals can be mischievous and unproductive.

Comparisons

Evaluation implies a criterion or multiple criteria. Normative comparisons from institutions which are comparable can help. Bases for selecting other campuses from which to request data (hopefully, forthcoming) are that one or several campuses have a comparable mission and curriculum, are of the same vintage, serve a similar clientele, have approximately the same resources and are in a comparable site, for example, city or small town.

The process of drawing inferences by juxtaposing local and comparative data is not automatic. Rarely are institutions exactly comparable, and so there is an inevitable need for inferences. Even so, the comparability of faculty resources, teaching loads and salaries, for example, can be highly informative.

Less valuable are inter-unit comparisons on the same campus. The reasons include the probability that some differences are the consequences of major and demonstrable factors such as curriculum, clientele and objectives. Another reason is that some interdepartmental differences express local decisions about allocating finite resources. An extreme example of logical differences is the difference in equipment funds allocated to a history and to a physics department on the same campus. Departments with research missions can consume a boundless amount of resources for computing and for up-to-date equipment.

Recommendations

The serious, time- and resource-consuming process of evaluation is justified in part by the opportunity to develop plans for the future. The content of a self-study is an excellent base on which a faculty may construct plans for the next several years. The plans themselves when presented in a self-study are more readily and efficiently appraised in light of the adjacent data. The faculty's recommendations for the future are grounded in detailed knowledge of their situation. We can expect recommendations on many topics. The mission, teaching, the curricula, research and service are obvious categories, and each may provide directions for faculty, other departments on whom plans are contingent, staff and students; relations with the community and, conceivably alumni when gift money is involved, are other examples. Such plans required reconciliation with the plans of colleges and of the campus.

When units are not experienced in self-analysis and planning, assignment of funds tends to be the hoped-for outcome. While not wholly unreasonable there are other considerations. For specialized units, periodic review raises the question of continuation or closure in light of their original missions and current status. Another aspect is that recommended changes may involve alterations in organization rather than resources. A department shrunken by retirements at a time of fiscal stress may merit incorporation into an adjacent unit if disciplinary boundaries are soft; on the other hand, a curriculum which has a substantial faculty and students may merit autonomy. Recommendations in such matters require reconciliation of unit and (for example) school or college perspectives. A campus-wide body may lend the necessary perspective.

Replication

An important aspect of designing evaluation studies is attention to the possibility of confirming findings by repeating the investigation. The process of duplicating the essential features of a study is called replication. It does not necessarily entail the entire process of contacting students and teachers and repeating every phrase. The critical elements can be attended to by dividing the data and repeating the statistical analyses. In chapter 7 I present an example in which data were analyzed twice. In the first case, there were 400 cases employed, and in the second instance the original 400 were supplemented by a further 200, a 50 per cent infusion of new data. This constituted semi-replication, a step which falls short of full replication—due to procedural matters—but which represents an attempt to vary the data set for analysis by introducing new subjects. An alternative is to use two groups of equal size or, conceivably, of different size but large enough to merit confidence.

The value of replication lies in the attempt to avoid accepting a falsely significant finding. If the original finding is statistically significant and is replicated in a second analysis we can be sure that the observation stands as empirically useful. When the analysis is complex (i.e. multivariate) the probability of confirmation tends to be less certain. When the explanatory value of an analysis is low, although one variable may be highly significant in a statistical sense, it strengthens our sense of practical significance when a repetition yields the same statistical significance for the same variable.

It should be borne in mind in evaluation studies that we are reaching for conclusions and evaluative statements using best evidence. In the last analysis an enquiring mind strives for firm and stable beliefs, and for practical conclusions. When the enterprise is complex, like higher education, statistics carry us only so far. Beyond that point reason, honesty and a sense of proportion based on informed sensibilities leads us to conclusions. Beyond them, the same spirit leads us on to recommendations for improving, reducing or continuing support for human enterprises.

Design

All evaluation exercises are experiments; that is, they consist of a question and a methodology in which data are generated and analyzed. Rarely we do engage in what is, misleadingly, called a 'true' experiment. That is a situation in which a series of 'treatments' are applied to people and the outcomes compared. For colleges that would mean that we said some people have to go to college, and we specified which, while also saying some people must not go—a control group. In practice we use quasi-experimental designs; that is, we accept that people have assigned themselves to treatments by selecting a particular college and, subsequently, a major field of study. The college experience is a treatment of subjects analogous to how much fertilizer an agronomist might put on a strain of potatoes or corn.

In the ideal experiment we test before and after the treatment, i.e. when entering and leaving college. Entering can mean data when leaving high school or when a Freshman in college. After college can mean at the point of graduation, or any time after graduation. This last interpretation can extend over many decades; however, it has connotations of significance and we will attend to them a little later in this work. The ideal design would be a matter of random assignment to one of several colleges, or no college, plus pre- and post-testing. In fact, post-college comparisons are not without value, although they lack the power of the best designs. They allow us to test one college major against another, and permit comparisons for different kinds of students.

Outcomes of Assessment

There are several outcomes of assessment and they too may be conceived at several levels. For private colleges and universities, the Board of Trustees may conclude that income projection and traditional goals need reconciliation. Raising fees may be impractical since increases rise until offset by declining enrollments. Assessment of the entire campus can identify centers of enrollment and profit, i.e. programs which attract students and gift money, and indicate that resources should be transferred there. Of course, campus level assessment in this style only provides answers to previously formulated questions, for example, well expressed purposes for undertaking assessment. In that sense assessment is a tool of planners, and planning exercises require a great deal of skill if private colleges are to prosper.

For public colleges much of what has just been said also applies, with the addition in many states of another level of review. A State board or system board may be superseded by a State governmental review, and they vary from requesting summaries of campus documents to undertaking separate reviews. The latter may be full-scale with site visitors or merely statistical summaries of costs per student credit hour, number of instructional days, number of graduates and secondary ratios of one item to another, for example, student credit hours/per square foot; the latter is a meaningless computation, of course, but statistical summaries as a mode of program or discipline review tend to miss the point anyway. State government may use statistical summaries positively, as in the case of attempting to forecast the future supply of elementary school teachers or podiatrists. A second positive case is when statistics are used to advocate program expansion where there are evident shortages of specialists.

At the departmental level, assessment tends to lead to a degree of self-consciousness about the quality of teaching, resources and program needs. It goes without saying that more resources are usually called for, but data provide a basis for deciding where priorities should lead us. In some instances, a merger with a larger department or another small department in a related field may be an outcome. Occasionally, spinning-off a program into a separate department is appropriate. Perhaps most useful is the opportunity to assess the curriculum in terms of student satisfaction and achievement. The latter may take the form of grades, of performance on achievement tests or on entry tests for graduate study. In selected instances, the salaries of graduates may provide an empirical test of their worth. At the least, their self-reported satisfaction with jobs obtained can be relevant.

The Disciplines

In the matter of evaluating specific fields on a given campus, comparisons can be made from accounting to zoology. For every unit we can develop ratings for the components of activity common to all. Among them is the quality of teaching which can be appraised by student ratings and by standardized observation scales. At the end of chapter 4 is a description of observable events in a classroom. The scholarly or creative productivity of the faculty can be assessed by counting research funds generated off-campus and rating publication of books, research reports and essays in refereed national journals. For some units, links to community or industry are relevant, and they can be appraised, as Benoit (1987) has indicated.

A more valuable exercise, however, is to enquire into how a given department compares with other departments dealing with the same subject on comparable campuses. Thus, it is helpful to know how well a social work program in a city compares to that of similar-sized campuses in other cities. In the case of the less applied fields appraisals of published research are a useful index of vitality, especially when campuses offer the MA and PhD. The curricula for these two degrees must be dynamic, and publication records set the stage for inducing a vital intellectual life in graduate students. From time to time, scholars draw up lists of departments using publication in prestigious journals as an index of quality. For example, in 1983, John L. Foster reported the number of publications in seven important political science journals, adjusting the number to take into account the size of the faculty. He reported that the top five universities in the matter of publications were Michigan, Kentucky, Texas A & M, Georgia and Wisconsin-Madison. This appraisal tells us nothing about the quality of teaching or of the amount of knowledge demonstrable by their graduates. However, it tells us that the faculties were active in scholarship, and we may reasonably infer that students were receiving up to the minute items of information in their classes; indeed, specific pieces of information would be imparted to students before political scientists in general have read them in the journals. In the field of economics, Hogan (1981) examined the quality of graduate training leading to the PhD in thirty-six programs. In an empirical study, the investigator used the publication activity of PhD recipients as the dependent or criterion measure. Two variables which were statistically significant antecedents were the research activity of the faculty and the quality of students admitted to the thirty-six programs.

The value ascribed by academics to publication as an index of quality is demonstrated in a report by Havran (1987). He reported that the American Council of Learned Societies' Board of Directors undertook to identify master teachers. They could think of no practical way to do so without taking into consideration the publications of the candidates. The quality of teaching can be evident in the written word long after the teacher has left classrooms forever.

In the related field of public administration Morgan *et al.* (1981) studied public affairs programs in 118 schools (out of 216 originally contacted). The objective component of journal publications, which excluded books, was studied by counting publications in ten journals. The relationship between the rankings of the two criteria of repute and productivity was not precise. Harvard University's reputation exceeded its productivity but, in general, fourteen schools appeared in the top twenty for both criteria. The authors pointed out that relationship between publications — productivity — and prestige is greatest in the natural sciences and less in fields which are more recently institutionalized.

A curious convention in the world of scholarship has been the use of ratings of campuses for quality in a series of national reports on selected arts and sciences disciplines across the nation. In 1966 Alan Cartter published ratings of 106 institutions. More analytically the ratings addressed six graduate disciplines in the humanities, six in the social sciences, eight in the biological sciences and five in the physical sciences and engineering. The institutions were rated from 'distinguished' to 'adequate'. This study, which pleased only those who came out well, was followed by the Roose and Andersen report in 1970. The number of disciplines expanded from Cartter's twenty-five to thirty-six, and a total of 2626 campus programs were examined. The results were much the same, with more people discomfited than pleased. One year later, Welch (1971) issued a similar study of programs in religion, a field not touched by either Cartter or Roose and Andersen. Welch visited fifty of the sixty-nine schools he appraised, but also drew heavily on the Roose–Andersen report for impressions. In a little known work Dolan (1976) provided a critique of the methodology. In 1982, Jones, Lindsey and Coggeshall published their appraisal of 'research–doctorate programs' in the humanities. They applied twelve criteria in the four domains, program size, characteristics of graduates, reputation and size of the library, to nine disciplines, art history, classics, English, French, German, linguistics, music, philosophy and Spanish. We shall probably have similar ratings in the future. The role of reputation in ratings is influential, and the rating reports contribute further to the mystique of higher education, but not to its serious appraisal.

For all graduate degree programs the rate of completion for students and the number of years from admission to hooding can be useful measures. In 1988, British research councils were reported to have set a completion rate of 70 per cent as the general good for completion of theses. Such figures are highly controversial (Turney, 1988).

Asking People

A method of assessment is to ask people what they think. This technique begins with ourselves when we make our plans for the day and assess the merits of driving highway A or highway B to work. Pollsters ask people questions all the time, and then summate the views of individuals according to background traits and sex. In 1985, the Opinion Research Corporation reported the attitude of the general public towards higher education over four years. In table 5 we see the picture which attitude testing revealed. The public thought well of higher education in 1982 when 72.5 per cent provided a rating of good or excellent. Four years later, in 1985, the percentage of responses in the top two categories of table 5 was 73.9 per cent. With regard to the public's sense of trend, nearly one half, 44.2 per cent, thought that college affairs were generally improving, in 1985.

We should keep in mind that the questions put by the interviewers dealt with higher education in general. They did not address a single question or a particular college. On the other hand, such generalized enquiries can tell us much about generalized attitudes and probably constitute a fair assessment of broad questions about quality and trends in quality. It seems not unreasonable that such questions could be put with profit by political science faculties to students on campus in order to register soundings of the campus climate and of the particular problems encountered by students.

Table 5: Public opinion of the overall quality of a college education in the United States: 1982 to 1985

	1982	1983	1984	1985
		Percentage responding		
Rating of the quality of a college education				
Excellent	16.9	13.5	15.6	15.5
Good	55.6	54.6	51.4	57.4
Fair	23.1	19.2	18.8	20.2
Poor	3.6	3.6	4.4	4.1
Don't know/no opinion	0.8	9.0	10.0	2.8
Trend in quality of a college education				
Generally improving, getting better	38.8	36.0	43.5	44.2
Staying about the same, not really changing	36.1	36.5	32.6	36.7
Generally declining, getting worse	23.6	16.7	13.3	15.6
Don't know/no opinion	1.5	10.8	10.6	3.5

Source: Opinion Research Corporation (1985) *American Attitudes Toward Higher Education 1985,* Princeton, NJ, copyrighted.

A related topic is the views of those who have completed their college years and can evaluate the entire experience after the fact, rather than in midstream. We now present such data.

Here are relevant, unstructured comments in 1986 from alumni who graduated five and ten years before. The goal was to derive in a subjective but conservative style an impression of satisfaction or dissatisfaction with the college experience from spontaneous prose. A space of sixteen lines was preceded by the instructions:

> *Please use the space provided to offer comments on the value you attach to your years at the University of Missouri-St Louis.*

The rating system provided for two degrees of positive affect and two degrees of negative affect. For comments which were not scoreable a zero was assigned. There were 163 written comments, of which 87.8 per cent were useable. Based on the scoring system, the proportion of negative comments from 143 alumni was 25.8 per cent, and the proportion of positive remarks was 74.2 per cent, a ratio 3:1 of favorable evaluations. By class some differences emerge; the class of 1981 provided 30.6 per cent negative responses, and the class of 1976 provided 20.6 per cent negative responses. The decrease in negative responses from the five- to the ten-year alumni is a substantial drop of 10 per cent. Reciprocally, the proportion of positive comments rose substantially from the five-year graduates to the ten-year group, i.e. from 68.3 per cent to 79.3 per cent (see table 10).

   From these results we conclude that alumni value their years of schooling on the St Louis campus of the University of Missouri, and do so increasingly, as the years since graduation increase. Here are examples of positive and negative comments.

Positive Comments

I feel that I received a well rounded education by attending UMSL, and I am grateful for the experiences I had, and the opportunities afforded me by spending four years at UMSL.

I feel my education at UMSL is very important. It is the reason I have been able to advance in my career. It is important to have a university in St Louis where middle income or lower income people can attend without undue financial hardship. UMSL fills this need in St Louis while offering a quality education.

I strongly feel that I received a top-notch education at UMSL. I was able to pursue business computer classes and foreign languages as I saw fit. Although, at the time, I disliked the requirement to enroll in mandatory liberal arts courses, I do acknowledge that I learned much about myself and others, as well as expanded my interests. The majority of instructors were highly professional, with few very poor exceptions. Since my entrance into the military, I have found little use for my MIS skills, but the general business courses and especially the languages, German and Russian, have been of tremendous assistance to myself and the US Army in Europe. I still remember the Russian classes taught by Ms G. very well.

At UMSL I found that the level of instruction was to challenge you and to make you think out a problem. The courses in business management, psychology, economics and physical science were the most helpful in my future career. They broadened my awareness of the world and helped me to better handle people as well as financial resources.

UMSL allowed me the flexibility needed to continue pursuing my education while working and supporting my family. Most faculty members were very supportive and helped to clarify life and career goals.

The time I spent at UMSL was a rounding out experience for me. The education that I received helped me to advance within the company. I was very satisfied with UMSL's educational system.

I feel my education at UMSL provided me with a wealth of knowledge, enabling me to live a richer and fuller life. I also feel that my training as an educator was valuable for my career as an elementary school teacher and was also thorough enough to provide the necessary educational background to obtain my masters.

During the years which (sic) I was an UMSL student I learned the value of time management. I was deeply involved in the activities on campus: working, attending classes and extra-curricular activities. I quickly learned to juggle activities in the given time span and was able to accomplish many things. This acquired talent has proven to be an asset for in the business world the ability to juggle various activities and accomplish tasks with relative speed is a definite plus. I am currently employed at the (deleted) Company, the highest paid Technical Specialist in the Manufacturing Division. I'm responsible for all the Office Automation Microcomputer VM network training for all of Manufacturing from the shop floor to the Vice President. UMSL prepared me for such a mammoth task. Thanks UMSL.

Negative Comments

At times I wonder if I wouldn't be better off having never gone to college. It's probably because I never applied my major of accounting toward a career and instead chose another field of endeavor in the business world as to why to this day my college degree has proven worthless to my business career. It has never opened a door for me in my career and at best, it has proven to be the butt of my employers' jokes as most of my employers never finished college and they ask me why I'm not doing better than them.

The problem with the school, as I perceive it, are the many classes with a large population. Large class sizes are okay for some type of courses, but inappropriate for most math and business courses. Besides making the subject more difficult to learn, at a school such as UMSL where most students are fron the local area and spend little time at the school except for classes, the large class size makes it more difficult to make friends and feel a part of the school. Another complaint I have concerned the homework load. Because most of the students at UMSL were from the local area, many also had jobs such as I. The homework load at times seems excessive. Without a doubt the homework load was greater at UMSL than at Mizzou where few of the students also worked. The fact that many students also work should be considered by the instructors.

Unfortunately I don't really place much value on my years at UMSL because I wasn't ready to go to college at the time — I just did it because I thought I should. I didn't try very hard and didn't know what to major in. If I had it all to do over, I would choose a different major, study harder and get more involved. However, I *am* glad to have a degree.

The aspect of my education at UMSL that I was disappointed with was the minimal amount of practical experience I received with reference to the real business world. I was able to acquire an abundance of theoretical knowledge, but was never given the opportunity to apply it to the real world, until I entered the business world. I feel an education should provide a mix of both theory and practice. The practice part of it was minimal. My education consisted of lecture and reading. I regret the university didn't tie in the practical aspect to better prepare me for the real world. I have a younger brother going through college now. He is given not only the chance to acquire knowledge, but also the opportunity to apply this knowledge, i.e., internships with companies, field studies. I feel he will be better prepared to face the real world with the knowledge gained than I was. I feel a person learns better by doing, than simply being lectured or by reading.

I feel at the college level—education should be designed closer to what the working world needs. There should be more programs that (sic) when a student graduates he is prepared to do a job.

One of the challenges in the life of a campus is to derive guides to improve academic and support services from the informed but frequently pointed comments of students and alumni. A useful step is to analyze statements for themes and for repeated, specific items. Consistent complaints provide an agenda for consideration. Not every comment is necessarily helpful. The student who believes that 'the real business world' should have been evident in the curriculum probably has a point. But we would need to know what aspect is most salient, and at what point the curriculum was least helpful. The reference to internships provides a hint which a faculty should certainly attend to.

Another method of defining quality in human affairs is to consult an authority. In 1987 Ernest L. Boyer of the Carnegie Foundation published his analysis of American higher education based on visits to thirty public and private colleges in a period of three years. Boyer's (1987) report concentrated on the undergraduate experience, and he provided a number of indices of quality. Among them he emphasized that a good undergraduate college:

— has a good mechanism in place for liaison with its feeder secondary schools;
— presents its program, goals and resources accurately and effectively to high school students;
— employs selection procedures which are honest and open;
— has developed a clear mission statement;
— takes great pains to make sure that the Freshman year is a unique experience;
— offers counseling and advisement all year round;
— retains one-half of its Freshmen;
— stresses the value of reading, writing and mastery of foreign languages;
— provides a coherent undergraduate curriculum which is common to all students and also provides for individuality;
— has a program for renewal of faculty;
— has a modest proportion of part-time faculty;
— promotes good teaching by means of student evaluations of teaching;
— provides opportunities in the curriculum for independent study;
— offers a full range of support services such as a good library,

microcomputers, study abroad, and a program of lectures and cultural events;
— generates a sense of service to others in students;
— assesses outcomes of the curriculum;
— undertakes assessments of alumni views and experiences;
— avoids a sharp demarcation between vocationalism and liberal education.

From such items we could set up a check-list to decide if an undergraduate institution is satisfactory. The problem is settling on the expert, and adding and deleting various topics. For some institutions major athletics has been incompatible with integrity; in such instances nothing short of dropping football and basketball will provide assurance of integrity. However, major inter-collegiate sports are a topic of such significance that changes may require a new board of trustees, a radical change in alumni attitudes, and reorganization of the structure of schools, colleges and athletics.

For graduate programs, an expert's list of indices of quality might begin with the provision of stipends for students above the poverty level, guaranteed remission of fees, money to attend professional meetings, a faculty with demonstrable research productivity currently, a library with breadth and depth sufficient to support serious research, and the dollar value of funded research in a recent year.

Of course, in the use of this approach the first step is to choose the expert to define the criteria. In fields where Nobel prizes are given the views of a Laureate would be invaluable. However, there is no necessary equivalence between knowledge of a particular field and knowledge about campuses as a whole. People can become experts in their fields without ever knowing that the campus instruction budget is structured by use of PCS codes (the Program Classification System developed by the National Center for Higher Education Management Systems).

Graduate Program Self-Assessment Service

Sponsored by the Council of Graduate Schools and the Educational Testing Service this evaluative technique consists of a pool of test items. Three questionnaires addressing faculty, students and alumni assess sixteen of nineteen possible domains; items within domains vary a little for Master's and Doctoral level programs. Students, faculty and alumni complete the questionnaires and the Educational Testing Service scores them. Common to MA and PhD programs, and with differing items, are the following domains:

Domain	Program level		Audience		
	Master's	*PhD*	*Faculty*	*Students*	*Alumni*
Environment for learning	★	★	★	★	★
Scholarly excellence	★	★	★	★	★
Quality of teaching	★	★	★	★	★
Faculty concern for students	★	★	★	★	★
Curriculum	★	★	★	★	★
Departmental procedures	★	★	★	★	★
Available resources	★	★	★	★	★
Student satisfaction	★	★		★	★
Assistantship-internship experiences	★	★		★	★
Faculty work environment	★	★	★		
Faculty research activities	★	★	★		
Faculty professional activities	★	★	★		
Resource accessibility	★			★	
Employment assistance	★				★
Faculty program involvement	★		★		
Faculty professional activities	★	★	★		
Student accomplishments	★				★
Quality of teaching		★		★	★
Faculty concern for students		★	★	★	★
Student commitment and motivation		★	★	★	
Departmental direction and performance		★	★		
Alumni dissertation experience		★			★
Value of educational experiences for employment		★			★

The domains listed from the ETS-CGS evaluation system, plus others, provide a preliminary list of topics to think about when planning evaluation programs.

An instance of the value of consulting experts is seen in the appraisal of assessment programs across the United States. From their week-long visits to five states, Colorado, Missouri, New Jersey, South Dakota and Virginia, Ewell and Boyer (1988) drew several conclusions. The major observation was the diversity of the five states. Virginia and New Jersey funded assessment well. Across the states the common elements were, the search for models, the critical need for effective communication, preoccupation with tests, the lack of a connection between assessment and other topics on the public agenda, the lack of synchrony between academic and governmental time lines and schedules.

In the public sector of higher education the overall question bruited at the moment is whether the customers got what they paid for. It does not matter how lofty the vendors' motives, how ivy-covered the campus, or how high or low the test scores, for the customer provides the empirical test of value. In Britian, in 1989, the Government's body for funding university higher educaton, the University Funding Council, deliberately conveyed through its membership a utilitarian emphasis. Under Kenneth Baker, the Secretary for Education and Science, the Council included a substantial number of people from business and industry (Tytler, 1988). The Government's goal was to bring market-place considerations into the question of how much money to assign to British universities and for which functions. Whatever the campus may decide about the quality of the product, the ultimate criterion, in the current idiom, is the satisfaction of the consumer, for 'the customer is always right'. The question is entirely fair, but methodology requires us to turn it into an operational form for which answers can be generated.

In the search for answers to questions of human valuation and development I am predisposed to a longitudinal design (Jordan, 1984 and 1987b). In the longitudinal idiom we appreciate that the baccalaureate degree is, in the words of Commencement speakers, 'not an ending, but a beginning'. That is, appraisal of the value of the college years is not necessarily appraised best when the speaker utters those sonorities. It is possible that the new graduate's evaluation will deepen in the world of work or further study. Accordingly, we should add to perceptions on Commencement Day the views of those who earned the Bachelor's degree some years before; time may add an important dimension to the evaluation of value received. From that premise an operational restriction emerges; it is that the datum sought consists of statements of value, perceptions and attitudes. What we do not seek is knowledge of particular gains between the Freshman and senior years. As sensible as achievement test data appear, at first glance, they are not without serious drawbacks as criteria. Some topics may not have been studied for three years when a general achievement test is demanded. Also, some subjects fade rapidly, for example, mathematics, from the brains of undergraduates. Finally, if post-graduation has any relevance, our chance of getting alumni to take achievement tests is virtually nil. At that point the choice of achievement tests at Commencement (a criterion for graduation?) versus assessment at Commencement plus subsequent time points acquires procedural as well as intellectual significance. In the original data I will report later in this work I emphasize the sense of value which alumni— customers—attribute to the educational product they purchased as undergraduates. Their appraisal of twenty-one aspects of their schooling is the datum of chapter 7.

Chapter 4

Evaluating the Academic Program

Assessing Mission Statements

One of the conventions of higher education is that campuses shall have mission statements. This is a brief text, usually no more than several paragraphs long, in which a college sets forth its raison d'être. Usually consisting of compound sentences overloaded with meaning, the mission statement attempts to do several things. One is to explain the high purposes of the campus and its contribution to the lives of students; it then proceeds in ever-widening scope to demonstrate its contribution to the local or national polity. At the same time the mission statement conveys what the campus feels is distinctive about its internal characteristics and vis-à-vis other institutions. An example is the unique mission to serve rural, and possibly urban, clienteles in a practical way, off-campus, accepted by land-grant institutions established in each state under the Morrill Act.

The goal of mission statements is to articulate both the values campuses propose to defend and advance, and the means they deem suitable to reach their goals. Accordingly, development and legitimation of mission statements is a vital step for colleges. Once phrased by appropriate constitutencies, usually faculty, students, alumni, administrators and staff, they are approved formally by appropriate boards, officials and agencies above the level of the campus chief executive officer. In practice, those giving final approval are free to change language in the process of development, thereby enlarging or restricting the scope of campus affairs.

It should be pointed out that campuses also have rules and regulations, and they express the mechanisms by which the philosophical ends of the mission statement are carried out. In addition, there may be mission statements developed by each department, school or college on campus. Normally, they provide the materials from which the broadest campus-wide statement of mission is formulated. A unit mission statement cannot contradict or exceed the campus mission statement, and so the process of development usually consists of broad consultation and reconciliation of language. This is a critical step in validation of a mission statement because the language will be invoked to justify or deny innovations.

Another parallel to the language of a campus mission statement is the formulation of specific goals for units. Here, the language is more concrete and describes the kinds of graduates units will develop. Students' skills, competencies and knowledge are set forth explicitly, and are usually linked as objectives to the broader campus mission statement. There is a limit to how far into the table of organization we can go; non-academic units tend not to have mission statements, although student affairs is a noticeable exception. But buildings and grounds, and financial offices tend to lack theoretical statements beyond their justification as necessary means on the table or organization.

In some respects goals and objectives for individual courses relate to mission statements. The linkage of particular courses is more likely to be with department goals than to the campus-level statement of mission. In religiously-affiliated schools, the linkage from campus mission to courses may be expressed by starting each class with a prayer, and by a self-conscious effort to use illustrations from scripture or anecdotes from the lives of saints and prophets. Teaching 'doctrine', a term employed in military colleges as well as in seminaries, is a way to express campus-level mission statements in specific courses. Of course, there are limits to how explicitly we can connect, for example, an urban mission statement to specific courses. For example, the periodic table of the elements and Greek irregular verbs resist attempts to give them an urban flavor as course content.

Management

From a campus point of view, mission statements are devices to expand programming and justify innovations. When the language of mission is ambitious and ennobling there is very little that is inappropriate. On the other hand, the era has passed when expansion can be unbridled; today, control of expansion is a minimum requirement, and the cost of higher education requires management of institutional change. Accordingly, mission statements can be viewed as premises for management, and as a series of statements against which innovations can be appraised. Tactically, the costs associated with innovations can also be appraised and placed in priority. In that respect a mission statement is a management plan in essence. Assessing a mission statement requires that the wording incorporate inhibitions as well as lofty ambitions. Little is gained by phrasing unattainable ambitions in an age of stability or modest expansion.

For public institutions, campus mission statements aggregate into a state-wide formulation. At that level, avoidance of unnecessary duplication, guarantee of access and prudent assignment of State funds add another level of concerns. Local ambitions frequently overlap, and so accountability to the public requires management decisions at variance with local objectives. An example is the prerogative for a campus to accept or reject transfer credits based on the local ideology. State legislators simply do not believe that campus autonomy in general education is justified. Accordingly, a State-level formulation of mission for public higher education usually requires that some coordination be obligatory. In New York state, some years ago, dismantling degree programs seemed necessary in the face of campus aspirations and demonstrable history. Campus missions, in that climate, appeared irreconcilable with a broader sense of the common welfare. Indeed, campuses may update their mission statements, but also retain a formulation of themselves and of society which is obsolete, and refracting a world we have lost.

A striking exception is the 1987 mission statement of North-east Missouri State University under the leadership of Dr Charles McClain (Ewell, 1987a). Here are the old and new — 1987 — statements illustrating a radical reconstruction of the vision of the campus:

Northeast Missouri State University Mission Statement
The Old vs. The New

The Old Mission

The New Mission

The mission statement of Northeast Missouri State University articulates the University's commitment to the advancement of knowledge, to the personal, social and intellectual growth of students, to the larger societal needs through service and to freedom of thought and enquiry. One common element in each of these purposes is the University's commitment to excellence as applicable to education.

Northeast Missouri State University is committed to the advancement of knowledge, to freedom of thought and enquiry, and to the personal, social, and intellectual growth of its students. The University strives to identify and maintain a universally recognized standard of excellence in all of its educational activities.

The mission of the University is to achieve excellence through (i) a liberal arts-based higher education; (ii) nationally competitive

The mission of Northeast Missouri State University is to offer an exemplary undergraduate education, grounded in the liberal preprofessional, professional, and career-oriented programs; (iii) selected graduate programs at the master and specialist levels in areas that have achieved excellence at the undergraduate level; (iv) pure and applied research efforts consistent with the teaching and public service functions of the University, (v) continuing education opportunities which meet national needs and are a public outgrowth of existing programs; and (vi) public service.

While the University must focus on the intellectual development of its students, it should also be certain that ample opportunities are provided for them to be engaged in experiences by which they can grow physically, psychologically, socially, and spiritually.

To accomplish its mission, the University must identify and meet the changing needs of North-east Missouri as well as the larger society of which it is a part. Preprofessional, professional and graduate programs, as well as continuing education opportunities, must take into consideration the realities of employment trends, expectations of the various constituencies and the aesthetic value of education, recognizing that the student needs not only to prepare for employment but also to live a full life.

arts and sciences, in the context of a public institution of higher learning. To that end the University offers undergraduate studies in the traditional arts and sciences, as well as selected preprofessional, professional and master's level programs that grow naturally out of the philosophy, values, content and desired outcomes of a liberal arts education.

The highest goals of a liberal arts education are to ignite the individual's curiosity about the natural and social universe and then aid him or her in developing the skills and personal resources to channel knowledge into productive, satisfying activity. In pursuing these goals, the University seeks to cultivate in its students:
(a) intellectual integrity, tolerance of difference and diversity, informed ethical values, and courageous aspiration toward the best for oneself, one's family, one's society and the world;
(b) a sense of the joys and uses of creative and critical thought, including skills of intellectual problem-solving through effective reading and research, lucid expository prose, and articulate speech;
(c) the willingness and ability to exercise personal and intellectual leadership in his/her chosen field of endeavor.

The University will achieve its mission through emphasizing and supporting excellence in teaching, in pure and applied research and in public service consistent with the educational emphases and goals of the University. In fulfilling this mission, North-east Missouri State University recognizes its duty to:
(a) maintain a living and learning environment that will attract and challenge outstanding students;
(b) prepare its students to succeed in rigorous professional and graduate programs;
(c) provide a physical environment and support services that will help members of the University achieve their educational goals and enhance their social and physical development and further

serve as a source of pride to the University, the alumni, the community and the state;

(d) offer services to the community, the region and the state in the areas of research and public service that are natural outgrowths of the academic mission of the University, and strive to ensure that the University serves as a cultural resource for the broader community of which it is an integral part;

(e) develop and maintain sources of public and private support, and merit such continued support through public accountability for the quality of its programs and resources;

(f) provide appropriate encouragement and recognition of each member of the University community who contributes to the fulfilment of the University's goals.

In the new statement we see the introduction of the liberal arts as the ethos of the campus. This is a decisive move away from the traditions accrued since the institution was opened in 1867, as the normal college for a rural region. The 1987 statement is more explicit than its predecessor in several areas and its idiom catches the flavor of the times in use of terms such as 'public accountability'. That innovation is entirely appropriate since North-east Missouri State University has been a leader in the process of increasing accountability in higher education to the public.

Rhetoric-vs-Practice

A little earlier, we introduced the notion of discrepancy. The topic can arise in the tension between rhetoric in mission statements and practical matters. Many mission statements address recruitment of a wide spectrum of students and also assert an interest in frugality. A discrepancy is inherent when campuses invest money in compensatory and preparatory programs for selected students who enter college ill-prepared. To the normal per capita cost of instruction is added the cost of special programs, counselors and other services. Wording mission statements carefully can help campuses avoid being hoisted by their own petard; incorporating references to 'appropriate costs' rather than simply stressing low costs can help. Access is another potential source of contradiction, especially at the State level, when technology and associated costs are concentrated on historic campuses to the detriment of newer campuses or actual centers of population. A third example is assignment of Federal extension funds to country campuses, and so to rural populations, when people have abandoned farming and moved to towns.

State-level mission statements for higher education need to anticipate the approaching twenty-first century rather than the nineteenth century. Reflecting that theme would be attention to telecommunications as a mode of delivering instruction in selected fields. A full appreciation of the times we live in suggests that some campuses have no defensible mission, and so merit merger into a more rational whole with one or more other institutions. No campus is likely to offer that conclusion, and some private institutions have sought new clienteles and geographic sites for service in recent decades. Like cuckoos which lay their eggs in other birds' nests, some institutions have formulated missions which lead them into other cities, states and even countries. Such ambitious missions are not easily reconciled with quality, but that state of affairs is comparable to public universities offering extension courses in rural areas without library resources. In terms of mission, some campuses will do a great deal to balance the budget and maintain enrollments. It follows that reading mission statements is an exercise in divination as we seek to identify advancement of the common welfare, the clientele and the geographic boundaries the campus acknowledges. We hope to identify a unique attribute, or ethos, for without one it seems unlikely that a campus can be distinguished from other campuses.

Meaning

There remains the fundamental question of validity in mission statements. Validity in this context draws on the correspondence theory of truth; that is, we ask if the mission corresponds to internal reality of campuses, resources and to the external reality of the larger world. The first portion of this approach asks if physical resources, faculty and finances are sufficient for the mission. The second portion asks if the target clientele really exists and if, for example, we need another MBA program in a metropolitan area.

Time has caught up with mission statements. Originally conceived in the tradition of American rhetoric in the nineteenth century, mission statements are no longer inspirational, slightly vague but hortatory statements of good intentions which uplift and inspire. Today, they are formulated as ways to convey the self-image and plans the campus values for the discernible future. As circumstances change so should the mission statement as a strategic, if not tactical, document. Timing the challenging task of developing or modifying a mission statement is a major task of leadership. Frequently, preparation for campus accreditation or a change of presidents sets the stage for the challenging, slow and difficult task of organizing the campus community. If the mission statement is to have the essential element of broad support, participants in the process of drafting and redrafting prose will have prolonged and occasionally tense sessions in which fine shades of meaning are exchanged. The outcome will be successful when the various constituencies have a sense of what the future holds for them. When emphases change and priorities rise and fall in the statement of mission it should be evident that resources will flow away from some programs and accrue in others. There should be a clear inference that a management plan will assess the extent to which redirection of resources has advanced the progress of the campus towards the goals of the mission statement. Communication of these points cannot be overemphasized since people tend to hear what they want to hear, and may react with amazement when changes foreshadowed in reports actually come about.

Student Achievement

At the heart of assessment on campuses is the topic of student achievement. In this work the importance of the matter is stressed by making it the subject of a separate section. Please turn to the appendix for a detailed presentation of measuring student achievement in the context of departmental instruction.

Assessment of Developmental Education

There is consensus that the college gates should not remain closed to young people who are ill-prepared when they leave secondary school. Not every student with low achievement is intellectually incapable of learning, but not every secondary school is responsible for the sorry state of adolescents who frittered away their opportunities. Developmental or remedial education is a treatment intended to improve the odds that selected Freshmen will survive. It may well be that the social support in such programs is a vital element to be appraised. Such programs are expensive and they represent assignment of funds away from the student body in general to assist entering students who are at risk. In 1981 Akst and Hecht estimated that New York's City University was spending $35m annually on developmental education. It seems reasonable for fiscal reasons to ask how productive investments in remedial education are, accordingly, whatever the scale of the investment. Apart from the financial cost per student there are collateral questions about the use of space, diversion of energy, and possible deception of students who may fantasize exotic occupational futures on their lack of knowledge. We need to be sure that remedial education is not a cruel hoax played on the unfortunate or on the unrealistic.

The evidence suggests that remedial education is not a waste of time. Kulik, Kulik and Schwalb (1983) conducted a meta-evaluation of sixty studies on the effectiveness of remedial education since 1935 (they note a study on the subject at Wellesley in 1894). The most frequent criterion of success was the grade point average (gpa), and former remedial students tended to have higher gpa's than control students. They also reported that research showed that former remedial students persisted in school longer than controls, although the opposite occasionally emerged.

Clearly, the focal question is, 'what shall be the criterion of success for remedial education?' The range of measures is quite wide and multiple criteria seemed called for. Of course, as in all evaluation we need a clear statement of the question or questions which the criteria are meant to illuminate. Some years ago, while working in remedial education, the writer and a colleague were asked to identify how many brilliant young people were being rescued by remedial education in reading and study skills. The enquiry revealed that there were no such rough diamonds among several hundred 18-year-olds. As with many evaluative exercises formal questions of a scientific nature may lead to questions such as, 'Shall we continue this program or put the money elsewhere?' 'Shall we invest more money and also enroll more students in developmental education?'

Criteria are lampposts to illuminate the data. Maxwell (1981) lists the following criteria for possible use.

1 Students' use of the service.
2 Students' satisfaction with the program.
3 GPA (note, this can take several forms).
4 Retention rates.
5 Test scores.
6 Attitudes of faculty towards the program (they know how well remedial students are doing).
7 Attitudes of people working in the remedial program.
8 Impact of the program on the campus.

Akst and Hecht (1981) favor summative evaluation and point to:

1 The appropriateness of the remedial program's objectives.
2 The relation of course content to the objectives.
3 The appropriateness of the assessment plan to the procedures selected.
4 The effectiveness of instruction.
5 The efficiciency of instruction.

These considerations are important as we begin to consider what we wish an evaluation plan to do. They help us decide what the desiderata are, and what are major and minor emphases. Boylan (1983) asserted that there are three questions which remedial-developmental education should be prepared to shed light on:

1 Do developmental programs actually improve the basic academic skills of those students who participate in them?
2 Do students who participate in developmental programs actually obtain higher grades following participation?
3 Do students who participate in developmental programs actually have higher rates of retention than those who do not?

The general tenor of evaluation addresses group data and emphasizes objective information. Walvekar (Hild, 1982) has four questions for learners who have been through remedial-developmental programs. She asks,

1 Do you feel more confident about your ability to read, write, study or solve problems? Why?
2 Are you interested in learning the subjects that you are studying this semester? How do you know?
3 Are you usually motivated to study for your courses?
4 When you are not motivated, what do you do to make yourself study?

The tone of these student-directed questions is not substantive but affective, and so recognizes that skill training may not be enough. There are many young people who distrust their ability to succeed, and so begin a downward spiral. In such cases, the core is not the IQ but the self-concept. Such is the plasticity of human nature that college-age young people are capable of great growth, but it tends to be of the accidental, self-prescribed variety. A program which supplements training in skill with attention to self-worth may be the way to guarantee the application of hard-earned skills.

Perhaps the important information a campus can learn is the boundary of effectiveness to remediation. Should the criterion for continuing a program be the proportion of students who graduate? The fact is that the graduation rate among non-remedial Freshmen can be surprisingly low four years later. It should be possible to estimate how much further than the first semester remedial students can be expected to get in their initial college experience. For better or ill, many students do not observe the four-year schedule to graduation. Remedial students probably share that trait, and may return to their studies in later years. In such cases the more we know from massed data the less we know about the idiosyncratic individual. However, remedial education has costs and we need to know how effective such programs are, by multiple criteria.

Evaluating Teaching and Research

Faculty

In the case of faculty, evaluation is usually an annual event. When the year has begun with a statement of personal goals, evaluation at the end of the year can draw on them as criteria. While specificity of faculty goals is a virtue, goals themselves may be only relatively suitable. On campuses where teaching and service are the prime functions the administrative act of assigning duties may provide the goals. The technique of setting student levels of achievement as goals for faculty is imprecise; it fails to take into account the previous preparation and present aptitude of students. While not wholly irrelevant, it should be used with flexibility, if at all. A useful form of teacher evaluation is to ask students to rate faculty on a variety of behaviors such as accessibility, command of the subject, fairness of tests, skill at classroom presentation, punctuality and use of varied instructional procedures such as lectures, discussions, assignments and instructional aids.

For research-oriented campuses faculty annual evaluation may or may not fit the cycle of scholarship. The enquiry may permit beginnings and endings within the span of the academic year; however it probably will not. Further, some projects require years to complete. The key is to understand scholarship as a process extending over time which is tentative and explanatory. While a research worker knows the general and specific compass points to seek, the act of beginning the research journey reveals new directions. Some pathways are productive and some are not. As a result the question of goals in research permits us to expect a tidy set of interim plans, but does not permit us to extend accountability literally to research objectives. In the matter of quality of what is achieved, it is usual to accept public presentation of results in journals as evidence. Journals vary in their regional-to-international scope, and rates of rejection for quite sound research papers may be high. It follows that qualitative assessment of research depends on the folkways of the disciplines. The research complex, at that point, is beyond local control, and the standards and practices of the disciplines prevail. Within the disciplines are variations in style; in some scientific fields results are boiled down to a page or two, while in others research over an equally long period of time may yield a book. Presentation of papers is also important, but it should, perhaps, be viewed as a trial run for a presentation in a scholarly journal. In the case of evaluation of research for promotion, it may be reasonable to expect to see a mature scholar produce a long manuscript offering a synthesis of findings and a reasoned set of observations. In the case of the creative arts the comparative tidiness of the sciences and most humanities is simply not relevant. Appraisal is much more subjective, but there must be something to appraise, as a starting point.

Evaluating Administrators

Administrators need assessment, and it usually comes from two perspectives. There is the view of the superior who judges quality, promptness and efficiency in human relations and administrative processes as demonstrably satisfactory or not. A second viewpoint is that the campus personnel who look to the administrator to make creative initiatives and generally keep the processes flowing. Typically, a superior will rate an administrator and also ask the faculty to rate the person. From the combination of superior and inferior perspectives, plus self-ratings, it is possible to arrive at a credible picture of an administrator's performance.

The higher up the academic administrative ladder we look the greater the need to shift from evaluation based on critical incidents, for example, budget crises, to evaluation in which the quality of far-reaching decisions is evident. Short-term decisions are relatively easy to make; it is the long-range implications of decisions for complex organizations which is unique for upper-level administrators.

At the lower level, for example, department chairpersons, campuses vary in their formulation of chairing. In large schools and colleges the responsibilities are like those of deans on smaller campuses. For both large and small units the role of chair tends to be part faculty, part administration. Given the practice of appointments for term, department chairs are sensitive to faculty relations, since they must live with their colleagues in an after-life. A good departmental chair will be a good manager, but also remain a practising teacher and scholar. Evaluation, accordingly, is a matter of appraising a set of functions which are not always reconcilable but which are vital to success of the academic program.

Some qualities of administrative style for which we can obtain ratings are the administrator's

- understanding of the place of the unit and its faculty, staff and students in the life of the campus and community;
- quality of leadership, i.e. initiation of new ventures and attention to important issues, projected to the audience;
- ability to specify goals for the unit and for individuals;
- level of skill in oral and written communication;
- ability to manage office personnel;
- the ethical nature of actions and decisions;
- demonstrable level of making decisions;
- demonstrable knowledge of higher education;
- personal qualities such as attentiveness and consideration;
- approachability and accessibility;
- clarity in conveying personal expectations to all constituents;
- skill at professional development of faculty and staff;
- demonstrated level of support for appropriate activities;
- compliance with affirmative action guidelines and procedures;
- effectiveness at managing existing resources and obtaining more resources;
- skill at maintaining effective and accurate records;
- ability to delegate authority;
- clarity with regard to the reward system, raises, etc.;
- collegiality — the willingness to consult when moving towards decisions.

A useful source of information on the legal and procedural aspects of evaluating administrators at all levels is the book by Seldin (1988).

Evaluating Off-Campus Programs

In an era of vanishing 18-year-olds colleges have sought to serve older adults and those who might attend college courses if the college were more convenient for travel. Off-campus programs may be offered for a group of students at their request or may consist, at the opposite extreme, of an active campus granting degrees in another country. As an abstract proposition, serving the public can be an explicit basis for the existence of a campus. The 1862 Morrill Act established land-grant colleges in every state, and they offer credit and non-credit instruction on a highly organized basis. Far more informal are the programs offered by small colleges in rural areas seeking to tap the population of an urban area. The educational consequences of these two orientations can be very different. In the case of the prime dimension of quality there is no reason why it should be less off-campus. However, practical aspects tend to militate against quality. Examples are the degree of control exercised by campus academic units over the appointment of instructors and the standards for admission of students.

Off-campus instruction may be infused with marketing concepts which militate against quality. Invoking the concept of service can lead to abuses such as low admission standards and absence of library facilities. Sometimes higher fees are involved and the profit motive is paramount. Blurring the picture is the tradition of non-credit instructions which, while valuable, can seem hard to reconcile with the purposes for which universities exist.

The impact of telecommunications as off-campus education has been considerable. The television screen is never 'out there' but always 'here' in the learner's perception. In that sense the living room and the classroom are indistinguishable, for the teacher addresses the learners one at a time— in their perception—and so education seems highly individualized. An asset of telecommunications is that they have eroded the on/off campus distinction; the concept of resident credit has been a casualty since it is reduced to a series of concepts such as the opportunity for interaction, association with a group, access to libraries and the opportunity for conferences with the instructor. The possibilities for benign use of telecommunications are scarcely glimpsed at this point. Theoretically, the best of anything in the world can be brought to students by tele-communications and satellites. Examining telecommunications is an important aspect of evaluating off-campus instruction.

Evaluating Centers

Center is a generic term used to designate a unit with limited but focused objectives. Research and training tend to be frequent but dissimilar objectives, and such units may have no teaching functions. As with other units a clear mission statement is paramount so that criteria of effectiveness may be adduced.

Research units tend to be established to respond to a social need at the local or national level. Persistence or evaporation of that need is an important aspect of evaluation, since campus units tend to operate without a sunset provision in the documents which authorize their establishment. Evaluation of centers' raison d'être should be approached so as to require a conscious, positive decision to continue them.

In the matter of organization, the place on the table of campus organization merits attention. A campus-wide center should, demonstrably, draw on faculty from many units and serve many types of students if the unit is a service center for, for example, foreign students. A college-level center is more likely to be focused narrowly in all aspects.

For research centers, evaluation attends particularly to fiscal support. Synthetic fuels were once a critical topic, and centers addressing that question, while scientifically important, may not be supportable except in times of international crisis. In such instances the level of campus investment may not be great, and closing such a center is fairly easy since it will shrink progressively. Finance presents a quite different problem when federal or state funds of some size match campus contributions. The campus interest may well include the overhead funds which accompany the direct cost of contract research. Direct cost for salaries and equipment amounting to $1m may also bring to the campus a further $500,000 to cover rental of space and utilities. In some instances a campus may have an incentive policy which shares the overhead funds with the center; evaluation of that campus investment and its outcomes is a part of the fiscal evaluation. Another aspect is the proportion of campus to off-campus funds in the budget. As a center grows and increases foundation and federal support, the campus may reduce its investment in the center. Evaluation at that point becomes an assessment of campus philosophy as much as center practices since both elements appear in the center's budget.

Assessment of outcomes is tied to mission. For centers serving students the scope of programming, satisfaction of clients, the quantity of people served, and at what cost, are important items for which data can be provided. In the case of research centers, a list of publications, with emphasis on refereed outlets and books, is useful. Research centers should also be the basis for networking across the campus or college bringing together people who might otherwise not learn of their shared interests, skills and goals.

As a matter of procedure, use of specialists brought to campus to provide evaluative expertise is important. Properly chosen, such people can appraise a center against national and international standards. They can examine procedures for recruiting staff, assess management procedures and style of leadership, and evaluate the products and efficiency of a center.

Perhaps the most important outcome of an evaluation is facing the decision of whether to continue, expand, modify or close a center. Decisions to close usually require a period of time to reassign personnel and complete outstanding obligations.

Evaluating Libraries

Libraries

Central to the life of any campus is the library; the term is used generically since holdings may be in several buildings in order to cope with the sheer size of campuses, the number of patrons and to focus on the specialized interests of faculty and students. In 1988, the American Library Association revised its standards of 1979, addressing the topics of potential users of the standards and their objectives and needs. They reasoned that several bodies needed to know how well a library is functioning, whether it is supported adequately and its comparative status; all of these items were approached flexibly with recognition that local circumstances must shape an evaluation. The following topics shape the Association's standards.

1 *Underlying assumptions*: The library is a major investment, it is influenced by its local role, but is part of a wider information matrix.
2 *Goals*: There should be a set of written goals developed by a range of campus and other stake-holders working within a planning process whose achievements are evaluated from time to time.
3 *Important elements*: Budget, people, collections, development of resources, programs and services, university-wide relations, cooperative programs and responsiveness to change (for example, technology and innovation).
4 *Measuring outcomes*: A variety of people should participate in periodic reviews which should culminate in a formal document.
5 *Evaluative criteria*: The Association proposed the following forty-two questions in seven areas to guide evaluation of a library service:

  1 Adequacy of Budget
    (a) Are the budgetary resources sufficient to support current activities and provide for future development?

    (b) Does the budget support the purchase of or access to the necessary range of library materials?

    (c) Does the budget support appropriate numbers and kinds of staff for the programs offered?

    (d) Does the budget provide adequate support for other operating expenses?

    (e) Does the budget provide adequate support for new programs and innovations?

    (f) Does the process by which the budget is developed allow for appropriate consultation?

    (g) Does the library director have the appropriate level of discretion and control over the expenditure of the allocated budget?

2 Adequacy of Collection
    (a) Is there a written policy for managing the collection?
    (b) Does this policy address issues of user satisfaction?
    (c) Is there provision for considering change in academic needs?
    (d) What basis is used for determining collection levels and sizes?
    (e) Is there evidence of areas of undersupply?
    (f) Is there evidence of areas of oversupply?
    (g) Does the collection match the academic programs?
    (h) Is the collection growing at an appropriate rate?

3 Adequacy of Buildings and Equipment
    (a) Are the buildings sufficient to house staff and collections?
    (b) Are the buildings adequately maintained?
    (c) Are there appropriate space plans?
    (d) Is there appropriate provision for use by the handicapped?
    (e) Is the range, quality, and location of equipment adequate to the programs offered?
    (f) Is the equipment adequately maintained?
    (g) Is there budgetary provision for upgrading, repair or replacement?
    (h) Is there evidence of planning for the use of new and improved technologies?

4 Access and Availability
    (a) Are the policies governing access and use clearly stated and readily available?
    (b) Are the bibliographic records appropriate?
    (c) Are the collections properly housed?
    (d) Are the collections actually accessible and available?

(e) How readily can the library provide materials not owned?
(f) Is the staff provided for technical services and other collection-related services sufficient for the task?

5 Preservation and Conservation
(a) Does the library have proper environmental controls?
(b) Does the library have an emergency plan?
(c) Does the library budget have adequate provision for the preservation and repair of damaged, aged and brittle books?
(d) Does the library have adequate safeguards against loss, mutilation, and theft?

6 Resource Usage
(a) What are the library policies for resource use?
(b) How much is the collection used?
(c) How well is the collection used?
(d) What is the fulfilment rate?
(e) What is the relationship between collection size, collection growth rate, and collection use?

7 Adequacy of Services
(a) What range of services is offered, over what ranges of times?
(b) Are the locations where services are offered adequate to the purpose?
(c) What statistics and other measures of quality and quantity are maintained?
(d) Is the size and distribution of public service staff adequate for the numbers and kinds of users?

By emphasizing questions rather than explicit criteria, for example, not specifying a number of books per student, the Association's standards encourage attention to the role of library services and their nature on the campus. Within that latitude a library may be the traditional Greek-porticoed temple containing books and journals, a multi-media center or a books–cum–computers agency in which access to knowledge in all forms is the theme. The place of the library on campus is not specified, so that it may stand independently or be part of a complex including a radio, television and printing services. Finally, the standards leave unspecified the relationship between library staff and other non-students. It is left to the campus to decide if librarians, especially those with MLS degrees, have academic appointments. In general, the standards are broad and flexible and can help a campus improve its library.

Teaching Assistants

One of the processes of higher education in the United States is the continuation of a model of instruction which students are familiar with from their days in secondary school. It is the structure of education in groups which meet in classrooms. There are alternatives, such as tele-communications, but teachers and classrooms prevail at the moment. Staffing the many sections of Freshman courses is difficult, and the level of technical competence required of the teacher may not be great. Into the breach departments place teaching assistants, usually graduate students pursuing advanced degrees in the field they teach. They tend to be plentiful, with particular exceptions, and they are not well paid. On some campuses such people may teach for several years, but they may start out as discussion leaders, lab. assistants, graders, and attendance-checkers. The assessment of the scope of their use, the quality of teaching, and the perceptions of students are vital, timely topics in higher education today.

In an ideal progression, the teaching assistant is an apprentice who, as an Assistant Professor with a PhD in years to come, will teach effectively. In that mode, departments train graduate students to teach, monitor their progress, and provide duties of increasing responsibility and autonomy. Large universities such as Ohio State University operate agencies to prepare assistants to teach as well as to improve instruction generally (Chism, 1987). Complicating the situation is the use of graduate students whose first language is not English. Some campuses require both oral language training as well as preparation to teach from overseas graduate students.

From the point of view of evaluation the first topic is the nature and scope of using teaching assistants. Beyond the numbers are the questions of:

(i) level of preparation
(ii) teaching effectiveness
(iii) language skills (oral)
(iv) student reactions
(v) student performance
(vi) organized programs for teaching assistants
(vii) language screening and training

Addressing these and related items is a vital part of assessing instruction on campus.

Foreign Students

Evaluating campus services for foreign students is a topic of considerable importance. In any year many foreign students attend American campuses. For 1987/88, the Institute of International Education reported that 356,190 foreign students attended college across the United States (Open Doors, 1988). Half of them came from Asia, and Taiwan sent 26,660, while the People's Republic of China sent 25,170; India and Korea followed with identical numbers of 21,010 students, and Malaysia and Japan followed with 19,480 and 18,050 students respectively. The proportion of students from Africa and the Middle East declined, and the drop in students from Nigeria was the largest. On the other hand, the number of European students rose by 7.4 per cent to 38,820. The most popular field of study continues to be engineering, and business and management was next in popularity. In 1987/88, the five universities with broadest representation from abroad were the University of Arizona, American University (Washington, DC), George Washington University (Washington, DC), the University of Maryland (College Park) and Boston University. Most foreign students are enrolled in graduate programs, and the proportion of women continues to rise. The largest enrollments of foreign students are found in the states of California (n=49,197) and New York (n=34,693).

We begin with the nature of the preparation of the students before leaving home. Campuses usually require non–native speakers of English to present TOEFL scores (Test of English as a Foreign Language) which assess reading and writing. Most campuses require a test of spoken English (for example, the SPEAK test) and a training program for students who may become teaching assistants. There are states which now have laws governing the language and cultural orientation of graduate students who might teach. Some students are Canadians speaking English who have little difficulty merging into the student body and usually adjust very well. At the other extreme are graduate students from the People's Republic of China who are very bright but who may experience a sense of cultural dislocation. For them English may be difficult, and a supporting network of fellow Chinese students may interfere with use of English and acculturation.

There should be a central point of contact on campus through which housing and enrollment can be planned. Also, such agencies usually provide orientation programs and training to improve spoken English. In the case of some countries, enrollment of their students is a government effort to create a cadre of technicians and specialists. Evaluation of the effectiveness of the campus may be understood, in part, by the sponsoring government's degree of approval for the competence of the graduates.

In some respects, the prime criterion for evaluating the success of foreign student programs may be the personal and academic success of the students. To that end drop-out rates, grades and similar indices are appropriate. Organizationally, the degree of coordination of services may be the key. It should be possible to schematize a successful sequence from admission to graduation, with identification of steps needed to earn a degree. It should also be possible to list people and agencies ready to assist students; in that respect, the important thing is that the foreign students know that help is available and know where to get it. In that regard, informing foreign and domestic students is a process which never ends. For foreign students, much of the information may be communicated in their early days on campus when the ear may not be quite attuned to English. Repetition of information is a good way to be sure that students understand the services available to them. Their grasp of those facilities and resources is an important criterion for assessing a program designed to serve foreign students.

Classroom Practices

At some point, we should address the question of what actually transpires in a college classroom. Here is an observation checklist which can be used to describe the actions of lecturers and students; it also contains items relating to supplementary materials and to the interaction of students and teachers. It is not intended to be used normatively, although that application is not beyond possibility.

In the Classroom Observation Checklist there are three domains and there are eleven topics to observe and record. In I. *Classroom Organization*, there are four items structuring observation of how the class is conducted, i.e. the kind of activity, and when the class begins and ends. In II. *Teacher's Behavior*, we record the teacher in action, talking, moving, using devices, making eye contact etc. In III. *Teacher-Student Interaction,* we note what the students do and how teacher and students interact over the content, and how the teacher frames the opening and closing of the class. This system has proved useful in preparing graduate students to become teaching assistants, and may be useful in other contexts.

Feldman (1988) approached examination of what teachers and students expect to occur in classrooms through an examination of eighteen of thirty studies. He framed twenty-two dimensions of the classroom experience as follows:

1 Teacher's stimulation of interest in the course and its subject matter.
2 Teacher's enthusiasm (for subject or for teaching).
3 Teacher's knowledge of the subject.
4 Teacher's intellectual expansiveness (and intelligence).
5 Teacher's preparation; Organization of the course.
6 Clarity and understandableness.
7 Teacher's elocutionary skills.
8 Teacher's sensitivity to, and concern with, class level and progress.
9 Clarity of course objectives and requirements.
10 Nature and value of the course material (including its usefulness and relevance).
11 Nature and usefulness of supplementary materials and teaching aids.
12 Perceived outcome or impact of instruction.
13 Instructor's fairness; Impartiality of evaluation of students; Quality of examinations.
14 Personality characteristics ('personality') of the instructor.
15 Nature, quality and frequency of feedback from the teacher to students.
16 Teacher's encouragement of questions and discussion, and openness to opinions of others.
17 Intellectual challenge and encouragement of independent thought (by the teacher and the course).
18 Teacher's concern and respect for students; Friendliness of the teacher.
19 Teacher's availability and helpfulness.
20 Teacher motivates students to do their best; High standards of performance required.
21 Teacher's encouragement of self-initiated learning.
22 Teacher's productivity in research and related activities.

Given such degree of specificity about focal events in a classroom it is possible to develop ratings and checklists. Hypothetically, we could develop a parallel list of items about students for use by instructors in some, but not all, learning situations. Laboratory work and independent and creative activities are harder to snare in a taxonomy of learning behaviors, however. Jacobi, Astin and Ayala (1988) have summarized taxonomies of outcomes which people wish to see students achieve. They summarize taxonomies as a means from which researchers and practitioners may select items of relevance and importance.

Classroom Observation Schema

I Classroom Organization

1 Type of class: Lecture_____   Help session _____
Discussion _____   Charts _____
Lecture-Discussion _____   Recorder _____
Laboratory _____   Other _____
Tutorial _____   (specify)

2 Teacher arrives early

Teacher speaks with
students before class

_____ _____   _____ _____
Yes   No   Yes   No

Teacher starts on time

Teacher starts late

_____ _____   _____ _____
Yes   No   Yes   No

3 Teacher begins with goals and
objectives

Teacher ends with
assignment

_____ _____   _____ _____
Yes   No   Yes   No

4 Teacher ends early

Teacher ends late

_____ _____   _____ _____
Yes   No   Yes   No

Teacher speaks with students after class   _____ _____
Yes   No

II Teacher's Behavior

5 <u>Voice</u>

Talking _____ _____ _____   Enunciation _____ _____ _____
slow average fast   clear average poor

Pitch _____ _____   Loudness _____ _____ _____
monotone varied   too quiet satisfactory too loud

6 <u>Body language</u>

Eye contact _____ _____ _____   Gestures _____ _____ _____
little suitable much   few adequate too many

Mobility: Teacher
moves _____ _____ _____
none some a lot

7 Aids to instruction: Uses blackboard _____ times, and faces class ____ __
  1 2 3 4 5 6 7 8 9 10 +   Yes No

Uses other aids:
papers   ____ ____   projector ____ ____
        Yes No   Yes No

T V   ____ ____   movie ____ ____
        Yes No   Yes No

III. Teacher-Student Interaction

8 Student questions   1 2 3 4 5 6 7 8 9
                    10 11 12 13 14 15 16 17 18
                    19 20 21 or more

Teacher answers _____ _____ _____
              well adequately poorly

9 Teacher questions   1 2 3 4 5 6 7 8 9
                    10 11 12 13 14 15 16 17 18
                    19 20 21 or more

Student answers _____ _____ _____
              well adequately poorly

10 Teacher begins with   Teacher ends with
   goals or purposes   summary
       ____ ____   ____ ____
       Yes No   Yes No

11 Rating of teacher-student rapport _____ _____ _____
                              low medium high

Length of class _____ minutes

Additional comments
_____
_____
_____
_____
_____
_____
_____
_____
_____
_____

Chapter 5

Evaluating Support Elements

Strategic Planning

Strategic planning is the unending process by which a campus brings together its aspirations and projected resources into a single, integrated set of activities. It covers non-academic as well as academic components of campus life, and it is validated by the governance processes of the campus.

On the basis of demonstrable need, units propose activities in formal papers. For each item, there is a description, a statement of need, timelines, a list of intended outcomes and a description of how the effectiveness of the topic can be assessed at a later date. Matching the substance is a set of financial considerations consisting of full cost (there are no innovations without cost), the timelines for those costs listing increments by year, and the projected source of funds in each year. Some funds may be anticipated from reallocation, from fees, from gifts, from fee income and from overheads on research and similar contracts.

Evaluating the adequacy of a strategic plan consists of scrutinizing the elements. We ask if the costs are understated, if the need is real, and if the projected income in a specified year is trustworthy. Of course, retroactive appraisal is the best, in the sense that hindsight is 20/20 vision; on the other hand, actual expenditures viewed after several years can be compared with projected expenditures.

A key concept in strategic planning is that plans should be updated annually. Each year sees items funded, and so another year is added at the front as items are completed at the back. In that model, a program whose goals have been implemented receives no further funds (except campus-wide increments), and other programs come into the plan to be succeeded in turn by yet other plans across the years. Given the long-range perspective, some enterprises are intended to be for term, and so be excluded from budget support. Accordingly, review of programs and non-academic activities on a timely basis becomes vital in order to connect planning with operations and expenditures. However, connecting program evaluation to the budgetary process is not easy, and may be hard to demonstrate. An excellent guide to understanding what strategic planning is, and is not, in higher education is the work of Norris and Poulton (1987). Once we grasp what the elements are, we can then evaluate them in a specific campus context. Planning comprehensive self-study for accreditation is an example of a process which tells us a good deal about planning which has been in place on a campus.

Accreditation

Accreditation is the process by which higher education accepts the responsibility to police itself. According to Harcleroad (1980) accreditation has nine functions:

   (i) certifying that an institution has met established standards;
   (ii) assisting prospective students in identifying acceptable situations;
   (iii) assisting institutions in determining the acceptability of transfer credits;
   (iv) helping to identify institutions and programs for the investment of public and private funds;
   (v) protecting an institution against harmful internal and external pressures;
   (vi) creating goals for self-improvement of weaker programs and stimulating a general raising of standards among educational institutions;
   (vii) involving the faculty and staff comprehensively in institutional evaluation and planning;
   (viii) establishing criteria for professional certification, licensure, and for upgrading courses offering such preparations;
   (ix) providing one of several considerations used as a basis for determining eligibility for federal assistance.

In 1987, Patricia Thrash of the North Central Association listed ten values of assessing outcomes incidental to the accreditation process; they are as follows:

   (i) it helps institutions be more aware of the consequences and impact of what they do;
   (ii) it improves planning and resource allocations at all levels;
   (iii) it is increasingly used by state governing boards and legislatures

as part of mandated procedures for program review, approval, and funding of public institutions;
(iv) it provides more accurate information for consumers;
(v) it is valuable to private institutions in building effective recruitment and retention programs in times of intense competition;
(vi) it demonstrates institutional success which increases effectiveness in obtaining grants and other funding;
(vii) it encourages institutional improvement for its own sake;
(viii) it assists in the recruitment of appropriate faculty;
(ix) it serves students by accurately indicating what they can expect;
(x) it promotes institutional accountability.

The structure of accreditation consists of a variety of accrediting bodies. There are the accrediting processes and standards of the professions, by which, for example, the medical schools appraise each other, and there are the states' accrediting bodies which approve teacher education programs; this last is interesting because it illustrates that there can be several accrediting bodies looking at a program. Indeed, for a campus as a whole there can be several dozen accrediting bodies each of which may press for the attention of those who assign funds Uehling (1987) gave the number of bodies engaged in accrediting components of a single, comprehensive campus as thirty-eight. At the capstone of the process is the Council on Postsecondary Accreditation (COPA), which accredits accrediting bodies. This last step ('Quis custodet ipsos custodes?') is necessary lest the professional accrediting bodies became too prescriptive in their appraisals and attempt to tell campuses how to run their affairs.

Regional Accreditation

The evaluation of higher education on a given campus occurs at intervals of about a decade, and usually takes the form of an appraisal by one of the regional associations, they are:

the North-west Association of Schools and Colleges
the New England Association of Schools and Colleges
the Southern Association of Colleges and Schools
the North Central Association of Colleges and Universities
the Western Association of Colleges and Universities
the Middle Atlantic Association of Schools and Colleges

These six associations are voluntary bodies and they are augmented by other accreditation bodies which address questions in narrower spheres.

The regional accrediting bodies approach evaluation of campuses fairly gingerly. The North Central Association views the campus as a partner in the process of appraisal. It does so by phrasing four general propositions which the campus is invited to address. The North Central Association expects that a campus:

(i)   has clear and publicly stated purposes, consistent with its mission and appropriate to a post-secondary educational institution;
(ii) has effectively organized adequate human, financial and physical resources into educational and other programs to accomplish its purposes;
(iii) is accomplishing its purposes; and
(iv) can continue to accomplish its purposes.

These four items are supplemented by statements explaining them in some detail. However, the North Central Association approach is a long way from a prescriptive list of how many books should be in a library, what the fee structure should be, or how many schools or colleges should exist. Assessment of the institution as a whole consists of inviting the President to organize a report in which the campus analyzes itself in light of the four evaluative criteria.

In contrast, the North-west Association sets forth in fifty-two pages eleven standards covering:

(i)   mission and goals;
(ii)   finance;
(iii) physical plant, materials and equipment;
(iv)   library and learning resources;
(v)   educational program;
(vi)   continuing education and special instructional activities;
(vii) instructional staff;
(viii) administration;
(ix)   students;
(x)   research;
(xi)   graduate program.

In the case of (ix), students, there are fifteen standards one of which — the ninth — describes the North-west Association's views on a campus bookstore. The passage addresses contents, prices and profits.

The Western Association of Schools and Colleges sets forth nine standards. They are:

(i) institutional integrity;
(ii) purposes;

   (iii) governance and administration;
   (iv) educational programs;
    (v) faculty and staff;
   (vi) library, computer and other learning resources;
  (vii) student services and student activities;
 (viii) physical resources;
   (ix) financial resources.

Each of these is specified in greater detail; for example, the second standard, purposes, has two components, 'clearly stated purposes', which has a further seven components, plus 'distinctive purposes', which has five components, for a total of twelve elements.

The New England Association of Schools and Colleges has sixteen postulates or 'requirements for affiliation'. Qualitative criteria are listed in the following twelve areas:

    (i) institutional mission and objectives;
   (ii) evaluation and planning;
  (iii) organization and governance;
   (iv) programs and instruction;
    (v) special activities;
   (vi) faculty;
  (vii) student services;
 (viii) library and learning resources;
   (ix) physical facilities;
    (x) financial resources;
   (xi) ethical practices;
  (xii) publications and advertising.

In the case of (iii) organization and governance, the New England Association asks, 'What are the characteristics and make-up of the board — for example, occupations of members, age, sex, degrees, length of service, etc.?' Under the same heading, the Association asks about administrators, 'What are the responsibilities of each principal administrative officer? Where are they described?'

The Middle Atlantic States Association of Colleges and Schools seeks 'characteristics of excellence in higher education', and does so by eschewing 'formulas for specific application', and seeks to avoid, 'endorsements of particular patterns of organization'. This Association addresses the following fifteen topics:

    (i) characteristics of excellence;
   (ii) mission goals and objectives;
  (iii) program and curricula;

    (iv) outcomes;
    (v) admissions;
    (vi) student services;
  (vii) the faculty;
 (viii) organization and administration;
   (ix) governing board;
    (x) planning, budgeting, accounting;
   (xi) library, learning resources;
  (xii) other resources;
 (xiii) plant and equipment;
 (xiv) innovation and experimentation;
  (xv) catalogs and other publications.

The Southern Association of Colleges and Schools surveys eleven states plus some specialized agencies in Latin America. At intervals of a decade campuses are required to examine themselves and then appraise their status and develop plans to be reported to the Association. The Southern Association sets forth the following elements for accreditation:

  I Institutional effectiveness
    (i) Planning and evaluation
    (ii) Institutional research
 II Educational programs
    1.1   Undergraduate admission
    1.2   Graduation requirements
    1.3   Undergraduate curriculum
    1.4   Undergraduate instruction
    2   Graduate programs
    2.1   Admission requirements
    2.2   Graduate curriculum
    3   Continuing education
    4   The faculty
    4.1   Selection of faculty
    4.2   Professional and scholarly preparation (specific expectations given)
    4.3   Faculty salaries
    4.4   Academic freedom and job security
    4.5   Professional growth
    4.6   Role of the faculty
    4.7   Faculty work loads
    4.8   Evaluation of faculty
    4.9   Part-time faculty
    4.10 Graduate teaching assistants

The association distinguishes between standards which campuses should observe and those which they must observe. The Southern Association emphasizes 'an overriding obligation of the institution to offer its students a sound education leading to a recognized certificate or degree'; beyond that essential point, an institution is free to 'pursue its established educational purpose'.

Accreditation of institutions, usually for a period of up to ten years, can be a powerful tool for assessing quality. The processes leading to a decision by the Associations are complex and expensive for campuses, but the outcomes can be recognition of merit and of particular strengths; on the other hand, the results can be less than hoped-for when institutions receive less than the maximum years possible, plus comments on aspects of campus life and organization which visitors consider deficient.

It is possible, as an academic exercise, to analyze the criteria of the regional accrediting associations. Some emphasize one thing while others stress something else. Criteria vary in specificity, as do procedures; for instance the Middle Atlantic States Association seems to emphasize the role of the Association's liaison person in the process, comparatively speaking. In contrast, the North Central Association's liaison person is less involved in the accreditation visit, and the chair of the visiting committee, who may be a campus President, has a strong leadership position. However, the commonalities are evident. Self-study, external appraisal and the absence of state or national government in the regional accreditation process are salient features.

Fundamentally, regional accreditation is similar in all parts of the United States. Undergirding the process at a national level are the standards which professional associations and Federal agencies require. The National Association of College and University Business Officers (NACUBO) brings together fiscal officers who endorse standards of business practice for all campuses. The Federal government's Office of Manpower and Budget (OMB) requires compliance with its regulations for auditing research contracts, for example, OMB regulation A-21, from all universities receiving funds. The latter is very concrete control of university operations, and demonstrates that while education in the United States does not draw on the National budget, as defense does, it yields a great deal of autonomy as the price for the national research dollar. Other examples are animal welfare and the protection of human subjects in research. In all these instances, regional accrediting agencies expect that national standards of operation will prevail, while not necessarily invoking such standards formally.

The normal process of regional accreditation provides that a team of nominally qualified people from campuses belonging to the Association visit the campus for several days, read the campus self-study, and make a recommendation for accreditation to the Association for a period of time, up to a decade. Much the same procedure applies to the professional school accrediting associations; that is, a process of self-study culminates in a report and a visit, and is followed by a report and a recommendation. The strength of the system lies in the campus formally reviewing itself, and the weakness lies in the individual competence of the visiting team members. Usually, they are a source of strength and confidence, but they are limited by their own experience. Lest these comments seem less than wholeheartedly enthusiastic they are preferable to accreditation by government. States accredit selected programs, and State bureaucracies recommend campus budgets to their legislatures. In some states the implicit power to evaluate covers public and private institutions; there are all shades of subtlety in the degree of authority over both classes of institution, sometimes based on financial aid to students.

Evaluation in this context frequently consists of what can be counted. Small numbers of graduates may suggest inefficiency even though a program of instruction may be mostly service courses. Providing courses to all students as a part of general education may produce a few majors who represent a highly efficient use of resources. The point here is that numerical evaluations are virtually the only kind which busy State bureaucracies can perform. Such appraisals are useful, but may miss the point. On the other hand, colleges have responded well to pressure for cost-accounting their programs. They have a competent grasp of where their expensive courses are, and they apply their budgets at a high level of efficiency.

Student Personnel Services

While some professors tend to think of students' college experience in terms of lectures and acquisition of skills, such activities occupy a portion of the students' day. The total student enters the laboratory, and the attentiveness of students to professors depends on much more than IQs and the level of attention even a spell-binding lecturer can summon up. Adjustment to campus life, and the degree of personal maturity students bring to large lecture halls and residential life, affect academic performance. It follows that evaluation of the non-academic, support services available to students is an important aspect of assessing the campus experience. The Council for the Advancement of Standards for Student Services (1986), a consortium of organizations, has developed guidelines for understanding services to students. The Council has published comments on the following sixteen aspects of student life outside the classroom:

> Academic advising
> Career planning and placement
> College unions
> Commuter student programs and services
> Counseling services
> Disabled student services
> Fraternity and sorority
> Housing and residential life programs
> Judicial programs and services
> Learning assitance programs
> Minority student programs and services
> Recreational sports
> Religious programs
> Research and evaluation
> Student activities
> Student orientation programs

For each of these topics, each clearly a complex of great sensitivity, the Council has generated statements on the following aspects:

> Mission
> Program
> Leadership and management
> Organization and administration
> Human resources
> Funding
> Facilities
> Legal responsibilities
> Equal opportunity, access and affirmative action
> Campus and community relations
> Multicultural programs and services
> Ethics

Finally, the Council adds the importance of evaluation, advising that student services be evaluated every five years. While not proposing standards, the Council also called attention to college health programs, food services, athletics and child care. The latter is a reflection of the changing college clientele as well as the needs of people working on the campus. People from infants to pensioners are found on campus today, and all require the highest standard of service.

It remains to point out that the diversity of campuses determines the scope of evaluation in a particular context. Residential life may be the convention on one campus, while another may cater wholly to commuters. Some students will be handicapped, as in the case of Gallaudet College in the District of Columbia which enrolls only students with serious hearing losses. Evaluation of student services, accordingly, depends a great deal on the make-up of the student body. As a second example, a commuter campus has a unique relationship to students, one which tends to be quite utilitarian. Commuters' needs are specialized since they tend, as undergraduates, to draw on home for some support. Also, they may bring a supportive network of fellow students to college, and so be less dependent on the need to make friends. Evaluating services for them calls up a unique set of criteria.

Student services can contribute to persistence in school by bright students who are not yet sure of their goals. We should recognize that high academic aptitude does not confer personal maturity; average and bright students benefit from an opportunity, for example, to use SIGI (System of Interactive Guidance and Information) as a way to clarify their objectives. The American pattern of liberal arts studies in the first two years probably avoids premature vocational choices, and certainly allows opportunities for reflection by those students who enter college with objectives clearly in mind.

At the extreme, student services can help students with the all-too-common problem of depression. Expressed in many ways, this invisible but pervasive mental health problem can lead to withdrawal, drug abuse and suicide. Students may be willing to seek help on campus who would not approach the family physician. At the very least, student services offer a helping hand to young people in a developmental stage of personal transition. Timely assessment of such services is vital and productive.

Evaluating Athletics

Originally conceived as a way to achieve physical health parallel to that of the growing mind, athletics has become a complex with a life of its own. On large campuses, athletics operates as a sophisticated enterprise occasionally paralleling the functions of the campus with its own public relations and fund-raising. To alumni, the athletic program may be the sole remaining link to days of yore, while faculty view with suspicion the sight of unbridled power and handsome resources. On smaller campuses, athletics may exclude major sports emphasizing intramural competition and minor sports in inter-campus competition. Clearly, no single set of considerations can cover the range of topics.

For the average campus, there may be much to gain by examining the place of athletics in campus organizations. We would like to see athletics:

   (i) reporting to an academic administrator;
  (ii) subject to campus fiscal controls;
 (iii) subject to an annual audit and annual public report;
 (iv) operated for the benefit of the students;
  (v) monitored by a faculty committee;
 (vi) committed to support women's activities and minor sports;
(vii) enrolling students in good academic standing who are:
    – making demonstrable progress towards degrees;
    – graduating at a satisfactory rate;
(viii) present a careful statement of the relationship between coaching staff and an academic department.

Inter-Institutional Cooperation

After decades of shrinking resources universities have come to see the merit of sharing resources, and of forming consortiums to attract more resources. The public is relatively sophisticated about higher education and no longer perceives campuses with quite the awe of previous generations. Indeed, urban clienteles see a scramble for enrollments in the advertising through which colleges pursue their targeted segment of the market. This mercantile idiom produces consumers who use their educational purchasing funds as if they were dealing with any other retailer. Maximum return and quality are items expected from their educational merchant. They expect to see a range of products, and colleges have reacted by introducing new degree programs. They have also augmented their resources by pooling them. Examples are sharing access to courses—but not necessarily to degree programs, joint purchases of expensive equipment and shared physical facilities. In these enterprises colleges operate from a niche they have defined for themselves in the spectrum of higher education services. A Dartmouth is not a community college, nor a Hayward State a Berkeley; each is certain of what it is, so that the trade-offs from inter-institutional cooperation can be examined.

In this section we address the question of how to understand and value the various forms of cooperation.

International Affairs

At the broadest, many campuses seek to represent the breadth of the modern world in the experience of students. One way is to develop an exchange program by which students at the same level of education, and faculty, spend a year on each other's campus. Perhaps the most attractive system to students is the year-abroad program, frequently in the junior year, in which American students live in a home campus-sponsored facility in, for example, Rome, and undergo a structured nine months of familiar instruction and travel. Another form of exchange is to bring foreign experts to campus for research consultations and lectures.

In evaluating the many forms of international cooperation it is helpful to start with a review of the original goals. The reason is that details of procedure tend to mature, to migrate to some extent, so that in any given year people may be quite satisfied with procedures, but they may have lost sight of the original goals. A vital element is that the original plan should require evaluation in a future, specified year. Reviewing a program may or may not be fulfilment of that original commitment; by examining the original goals we can decide whether this year's procedures are satisfactory beyond the immediate criterion of current lack of dissatisfaction. Appraisal of costs is a vital component in an era when currencies fluctuate. Into a year-by-year plan a major cost item such as purchase of property, as opposed to leasing, may glide. Whatever the validity and cost efficiency of a property offered at a bargain, such an investment contradicts a year-by-year approach to programming. A major component is assessing the views of students who are ending their period of study abroad, and of alumni who can look back on the experience with a little perspective.

Curricular Agreements

There are fields of study in which states may have insufficient demand to justify an expensive program. For all but major centers of population, examples are veterinary medicine, architecture and optometry. Such schools frequently exist in adjoining states, so that students enrolled in one public university may enroll at the professional school in a contiguous state, and vice versa. By that mechanism, one optometry school, for example, may serve two or more states. Between institutions in the same locale, agreement can allow an expensive or needed program to serve students from several campuses. At a more modest level access may be limited to courses. The entire concept of access to courses, it should be pointed out, is evolving in the face of technological innovations. Optical fiber networks can transmit pictures as well as digital data. Satellites can relay signals to and from distant places, and so bring programs originating at great distances, including other continents.

In stating this observation we introduce a note of caution since evaluation of inter-institutional cooperation in courses and programs may be evolving. Evaluation in the face of changing technology in computing tends to be difficult for the same reason. Accordingly, means need evaluation, but so may ends as we extend the possibilities of cooperation and communication. Ends or goals of cooperation should be evaluated for their timeliness, since entirely new goals may replace old ones before they have been met. That observation is not a reason for avoiding evaluation, but for making sure that evaluation endorses ends as well as means. On the limited basis of access to one or two courses at a nearby campus, curricular agreements may be pursued at the more mundane level of assessing outcomes and the adequacy of means. In such enquiry numbers of students, costs, and student outcomes of achievement and satisfaction are important.

A hazard sometimes encountered is use of a less demanding course at a nearby institution to meet a requirement of the home campus. Students may take a mathematics course at a community college in order to meet a home campus requirement. If one course is all that is needed, the outcome may be satisfactory. However, should a sequence be needed, the easier, off-campus first course may not prepare students for a second course taught only on the home campus. Elective courses are the best example of courses expeditiously taken elsewhere; they may also be cheaper. Of course, such strategies between two private sector colleges or two public colleges are probably equitable. When students approach the private/public boundary of colleges there may be fee differentials, and therefore income differentials, which can create tensions between campuses.

The word 'cooperation' is open to a variety of interpretations. In joint ventures it can mean cooperation between equals, but it can also connote one-sided meanings in which the partner is thought to accept a minor role implicitly. In cooperative curricula, it can mean drawing on the strengths of two or more faculties in which all share the costs equally. More commonly, it means that someone who has a program perceives someone else as a useful hand-maid or junior partner; the junior is useful because it represents access to a target population. To the have-nots cooperation may be a temporary stage presuming full equality, and leading to an autonomous program at some time in the future. Assessment of the word 'cooperation' begins with an assessment of the identity of meaning all partners ascribe to the term. Accordingly, evaluation of goals for clarity is a starting point, although people frequently seek to set forth only general goals lest the idea be nipped in the bud.

Research Cooperation

It makes sense for colleges to cooperate with libraries, museums, zoos and botanical gardens, for example, in the conduct of research. By sharing facilities, research workers and students can pursue joint funding, while also drawing on each other's libraries and special collections. Evaluation begins with a clear understanding of goals and then proceeds to enrollments, appraisal of student outcomes, and the relative burden of costs in relation to benefits. As in all cooperative arrangements what is sauce for the goose is not always sauce for the gander. An arrangement may or may not turn out to be beneficial to the same degree, but evidence may show that differential goals, unique to each institution, may provide satisfactory outcomes. For example, an association with a prestigious unit may be a tangible as well as intangible benefit to a university; its private, philanthropic partner may qualify for educational funds and so increase its instructional outreach, as a satisfactory outcome.

University-Industry Cooperation

To corporations with narrow, time-constrained research needs, drawing on a local campus for technical help may be sensible and frugal. University departments profit by contact with applied problems and the possibility of gifts of cash and surplus, but not obsolete, equipment. Given the range of relevant disciplines from engineering to medicine, some universities have organized institutes to promote contacts. Perhaps the leader in innovation has been the University of Salford, Manchester, whose structure has been reconfigured to reflect the relationship with British industry. It should be pointed out that industrial philanthropy is a delicate, self-serving enterprise. Multi-national companies tend to enhance their self-concept by funding prestigious universities, although more pedestrian universities may be providing their technical personnel. Evaluation begins with the Roman tag, 'Cui bono?'—to whose benefit.

The St Louis Technology Center is an example of an agency established under the sponsorship of several universities and the metropolitan alliance of business and corporate interests. The functions of the Center are to:

- develop new businesses with strong technology bases;
- stimulate the regional economy;
- provide benefits to regional universities and corporations several of which are multinationals with headquarters in St Louis.

The Technology Center serves product- or process-oriented businesses which possess a strong technology base and have a significant market potential. The Center's services are offered to businesses in the early stages of development. Typically, the client is an engineer or scientist with little experience in traditional management roles. The Center's programs are designed to assist individuals in the development of both their products and the businesses which will take those products to market. The Center provides an array of services that reduce start-up costs and ease administrative burdens, and also provides specific programs to facilitate businesses' growth. In the latter category are three important systems; first, there is a strategic planning process based on technology assessment, market research and competitive analysis; second, there are interim management services for promotion, marketing and sales; and third, the Center provides access to financing in both the conventional and equity markets.

In its third fiscal year of operation, the Center's clients had grown to 170 employees in the aggregate, with an annual payroll approaching $4m. Having commercialized forty-five products, annual sales approached $10m. An annual state investment of $400,000 leveraged $15m in private investments.

In the case of research parks the same questions arise concerning the quality and value of sponsorship. The name suggests a wholly research theme, but research parks tend to accept as tenants other clients whose presence might grow into a relationship with the university. The nature of the relationship tends not to be inspected too closely, since research parks represent investments in infrastructure which must be amortized; accordingly, it is fairly easy for a research park to become merely another real estate venture whose tenants are not engaged in manufacturing.

Research parks tend to grow slowly and may require more than a decade to reach maturity. Examples of successful research parks with benefits to universities are the Philadelphia Science Center and, in the United Kingdom, the Aston science park in Birmingham. Less urban are the Research Triangle in North Carolina and, in the United Kingdom, the Cambridge science park. The Stanford Research Park in California is probably the most successful, however. For each of these research parks there is a unique relationship to the sponsoring university. The park may be leased land whose return on investment is merely an expression of successful renting to light industry. At the other extreme is the hope for only scientific, non-polluting, corporations tied closely to university laboratories. Reality is somewhere in between, and expresses the constellation of local land costs, the phase in the economic cycle, and the relative university emphasis on a short-term cash return versus an emphasis on evolution of science and technology into marketable products. Evaluation clearly depends on the original goals and appraising their achievement over time.

University-Government Cooperation

Private and public universities look to the Federal government for support. It takes many forms including research contracts in the sciences, social sciences and engineering, for example. Guaranteed student loans and graduate Fellowships affect virtually every campus. Appraising the relationship starts with the reality that Federal assistance entails Federal controls. Government money is a component of virtually every projected campus budget, and with it comes compliance with regulations. They describe accounting procedures and the establishment of committees to monitor, for example, research using human beings, use of DNA, and non-discriminatory practices. In some respects there is nothing to calculate in relations with the government since Washington sets the rules. On the other hand, the government seeks advice, usually through notices in the Federal Register, about proposed regulations. Finally, it is little known that there is a powerful agency in Washington, the Office of Management and Budget (OMB) which sets forth rules which greatly affect campus procedures to manage research funds and conduct research.

College-Secondary School Cooperation

American universities are increasingly sensitive to the high schools which send students to them. To colleges with a national perspective cooperation for admission puts the college in good stead. The exception is their need for minority students in their undergraduate enrollments. For regional institutions, liaison with high schools is a recruiting device. It includes giving college credit courses for graduating seniors and trawling the ranks of juniors and seniors for the talented. There appears to be a trend to make contact earlier in the pre-collegiate years as colleges realize that the quality and type of entry Freshmen should not be left to chance. Here too, clarity of goals is vital, and timely appraisal of processes and outcomes is a practical step to make improvements. In many instances the prime goal is recruitment of students. In that context, the number of entering Freshmen from the targeted secondary school is an empirical outcome which can be counted. Incidental to the number of recruits is the associated cost per student recruited.

Evaluating University-Industry Relations

A topic of increasing interest to evaluators off- and on-campus is participation in efforts to stimulate economic growth (Powers, Powers, Betz and Aslanian, 1988). The university's partners in this understanding are many. In some instances it is other universities as scientific resources are pooled to attack a problem. A variation is when universities cooperate to form a research center, with business or government as a partner. Still another version is when a university cooperates directly with business. The traditional form, of course, is faculty acting as paid consultants.

In all of these undertakings evaluation begins with an understanding of the objectives. Unless they are clear the possibility for misunderstanding is enormous. Universities traditionally approach scientific undertakings in an open-ended way, knowing that research can take people into unplanned areas. Businesses are product-oriented and tend to seek specific outcomes with expiration dates in their plans. Reams (1986) has listed sixty-five items which contracts for university-business cooperation might include. Representative are items such as, administration, mechanisms for approval of topics for research, patents, reporting, indemnity sub-contracting and ways to settle disagreements. In the case of government as the university's partner the situation is more complicated. Laws enable and fund projects and so Federal regulations must be complied with. The Office of Management and Budget's A-21 and A-110 regulations require reporting in particular ways.

An imaginative form of cooperation arises when State and local government come together with public and private universities. Under that rubric the criteria of success tend to be broad, ranging from reporting creation of new jobs to retention of highly skilled faculty who might otherwise be lost to industry. For universities, the opportunity for faculty consulting and placement of graduate students is important. Incubator centers, such as the St Louis Technology Center, pursue the prime objective of developing scientific ideas into products in a businesslike way. In that context the number of successful new businesses — their positions and payroll — are obvious standards by which to evaluate the joint efforts of several public and private universities, State government and individual entrepreneurs.

Computers

Over the last several decades there have been several instructional innovations based on technology. Virtually all of them have not fulfilled their promise. One reason is that claims for them were excessive, and tape recorders, for example, gathered dust on the shelf, except in the language laboratory. The second reason is that teachers remained central to instruction. However, computers may be a more valuable auxiliary. The promise lies in the potential for evaluating achievement by presenting words and images. Testing can be terminal, at the point when college Seniors are about to graduate, but it can also arise earlier. Used in that fashion it can constitute an opportunity for diagnosis when used in conjunction with samples of, for example, writing, which demonstrate analysis and exposition. Computer-testing can also be used to assess the level of socialization into the culture which Freshmen present. The computer can provide a checklist of presumed experiences and so an advisor can record students' progress through experiences which we intend to be enlightening. We might set up a list of concepts such as the set presented by Hirsch and his colleagues (1987). Measurement of such concepts can be tested in privacy with the computer and its screen.

With its boundless memory, the computer which records grades and courses of each student can follow the progress of students on a sequence of diagnostic/achievement tests in each field and improve the quality of test items. Finally, recalling my bias towards longitudinal data, the computer can record test item scores of students year by year. Such prospective data can accumulate quickly, but its overriding virtue remains the potential for aggregation into significant data bases.

Use of computers in instruction is quite compatible with the experience of middle class adolescents. However, my research on adolescents leads to the suggestion that familiarity with terminals reflects social class levels; social class is probably a covariate for school districts with poorer children attending less well endowed schools. However, many colleges set computer literacy as an early goal for college Freshmen. A second logistical deficiency remains the generation gap which leaves college faculty far behind their students in computer literacy. Time will clear up this problem. However, even a computer–immune professor can use the diagnostic output of student assessment to fine tune a course.

Affirmative Action

One of the accepted principles of higher education is that the campus is an agent of social change. Historically, the campus has been the site on which people of diverse ethnic background can meet, work together and prepare to infuse the larger society with the skills of competent people from all backgrounds. Under the impetus of laws, society accepts that opportunity alone may not bring improvement at a pace parallel to the changes in society. In that respect, the rate of change on gender issues has probably been faster than that derived from ethnic and racial matters. The result has been that change based on opportunity alone has been superseded by change in which people try to move more affirmatively into cultural diversity of students and faculty. Today, campuses have programs designed to ensure that opportunities do not merely exist, but are created.

Evaluating affirmative action programs begins with asking if there is a formal program. In that formulation, someone is charged with responsibility, and there are goals and objectives. Recruiting students and faculty becomes a conscious part of every unit's objectives, and they too are enunciated. Success in minority recruitment is perhaps the most obvious criterion, although retention is not far behind. Another is the identification of minority people in jobs above the entry level in all components of the faculty and staff. As a backdrop to campus efforts is the place of law, and conformity of a campus to the specification which statutes present. Identification of funds to encourage departments to find candidates is an effective strategy. Another is development of mentor programs through which social support and personal identification are encouraged.

Business Operations

In one respect campuses resemble businesses; they are complex operations in which large sums of money circulate, come and go. Goods and services are purchased and people are hired, resign, and, in between, expect to be paid promptly. The National Association of College and University Business Officers (NACUBO) has issued a series of manuals over the years describing how a series of complex operations should flow (College, 1988). There, NACUBO describes a variety of activities and provides examples from college campuses. Here are topics which the NACUBO guides describe:

Administrative Management
- Organization charts for business and finance offices
- Space planning
- Management information systems
- Records management
- Risk management and insurance
- Patents
- Legal services
- Student financial aid
- Personnel administration

Business Management
- Purchasing goods and services
- Auxiliary enterprises (for example, bookstore)
- Facilities planning and construction
- Safety, security and law
- Transportation
- Telecommunications

Fiscal Management
- Endowment management
- Investment management
- Cash management
- Budgeting
- Auditing
- Indirect costs of research, etc.

Financial Accounting
- Current funds
- Loans and other funds
- Plant funds
- Financial reports

Purchasing is a specialized field and campus purchasing agenda have also set up guidelines (Mooney, 1985). There are useful pieces of information on relations with vendors, setting up specifications for purchases, establishing controls and organizing purchasing services.

Within both of the enterprises just described there are complexities which only the expert fully appreciates. Presumably, an evaluation of non-academic aspects of a campus will conform to what is conventional in the view of specialists on other campuses. Assuming that the books balance, there are lots of ways to implement sound principles and to organize human efforts. Campus review of procedures can draw on professional guidelines to begin the process of review. The technical documents alluded to previously would make excellent reading for people proposing to evaluate non-student aspects of campus life. Of course, business offices vary in their use of software packages, and so reviewers need to apply principles flexibly if only because new innovations in systems and procedures appear frequently.

Research Administration

In recent years, the importance attached to research administration has grown. The reasons include the increased importance of non-campus funds in the budget, the value of the accrued overhead ('profit') associated with research contracts and the need to ensure compliance with Federal regulations. On research-oriented campuses, the budget routinely includes an expectation, or projection, of funds to be garnered from foundation grants and government contracts for research. In the case of contract research, a budget consists of direct costs such as 0.5 of the principal investigator's salary and benefits, equipment and supplies; added to that amount is an overhead rate, or indirect cost — perhaps averaging 50 per cent of the direct cost — to pay for the campus facilities, heating and cooling and diffused campus costs. The campus, not the investigator, takes these funds, although a prudent President shares some fractions with the scholar and the department. The entire complex of the research enterprise requires conformity to Washington regulations protecting people and animals, storage of hazardous substances, and monitored expenditure of funds. Evaluation of these topics consists of examining campus practices for conformity to regulations and to good fiscal practice.

There is no single model by which to appraise research administration, beyond the reasonable expectation that functions and responsibilities are recorded in writing. Such specificity can help decide, for example, who manages gift money or grant money, and who may or may not contact potential donors and grantmakers. Research administration has an academic side and a fiscal side; on some campuses, the fiscal side is managed in the business office, but it might be handled by accountants not in the business office; the local culture is the context, and determines the pattern of staffing. However, it is traditional that the administrator be an academic, since research arises in an academic context, and there are scholarly issues which require the attention of published, funded scholars. No particular field provides the best research administrators, but the prevailing pattern of a campus, for example an emphasis on the biomedical disciplines, may require a representative of that complex on the office staff.

A research office is involved in relationships with academic units, and many of them treat campus funds. There is usually a faculty committee which allocates small sums of campus money for research. Another faculty committee protects the welfare of human subjects in research by giving permission to investigators who submit research plans. Still groups monitor radiation safety and proposals to use recombinant DNA in genetic research. A patent committee decides who should share in the benefits of products developed on campus.

Office functions include degrees of help to scholars developing research proposals. Such documents may be ten to 200 pages in length, so that help with typing and with text may be necessary. Related is the search for funding possibilities by visiting agencies and scanning the Federal Register. There are many in the sciences and engineering, but few in the humanities. There, some awards are made to scholars in their private capacity, not through the campus. It can be seen that evaluating research administration is not easy. Several programs funding research may have the same deadlines leading to tensions and pressure. Research offices can be handy lightning rods, or whipping boys, when faculty are late in submitting proposals for necessary review and recording in proposal data banks. Review of operations at intervals of several years through a process involving external consultants is prudent and effective.

Special Projects

From time to time, campuses are approached by benefactors who would like to see a pet project placed on campus. Such arrangements are fairly straightforward when space is all that is required, and when rent is paid or waived as a university contribution. On the other hand, sponsors may have in mind an arrangement in which campus sponsorship is the vital component; in that case, expectations and understandings need to be articulated to avoid surprises and bad feelings. Benefactors may arrange initial funding with the expectation that the campus will assume full responsibility for funding. Even when no such unfortunate presumption exists, and money is not a problem, there are issues to be addressed before concluding that the campus is the site for a project. Criteria which can help evaluate the merits of a proposed campus activity are as follows:

1 Does the project fall within the scope of the mission statement, and is there an evident intellectual component?
2 Is there a planning and evaluation procedure for deciding if the project belongs on campus?
3 Are there research possibilities in the venture?
4 Have campus evaluators identified a cadre of interested faculty, and a possible coordinator or administrator?
5 Is there a curriculum which the project can support?
6 Will sponsors accept a sunset provision by which the project will be evaluated for termination or continuation?
7 Can the campus participate without diverting resources from current and future projects?
8 Do sponsors accept that the project will be the property of the campus, and will conform to personnel, administrative and salary practices? Are they ready to relinquish major roles in policy and management to academic personnel?

Evaluating State Programs

In the public sector State government has a role in higher education. By legislative act, each state has a bureaucracy whose functions are prescribed. Usually, the state agency provides staff services to the governor and the legislature such as commenting on public campus' requests for funds and managing Federal pass-through funds and State scholarship funds to students. Programming is also central, and the state bureaucracy usually monitors campus expansionism. Ideally, the agency does not supervise private institutions, but eligibility of private colleges' students to receive public funds as loans or scholarships has dissolved the nominally wholly independent status of many institutions. As a result, there is a spectrum of independence ranging from eligibility to receive State funds to funding with a degree of State control over programs.

States vary in their degree of bureaucracy ranging from bureaucratic over-control to modest attempts at coordination. Traditionally, New York probably has the heaviest hand and California the most elaborate system. The result is a varied pattern of efficiency and cooperation roughly proportionate to the degree of state involvement. On the unassailable premises of protecting the public purse and promoting efficiency, campuses and State governments live in various degrees of stability and unanimity. As with all theoretical models the reality is tempered by personalities. Strong executives on campuses and in state capitols negotiate with weaker and stronger counterparts. In turn, their roles are modulated by the degree of attention paid by governors and legislative leaders. It follows that evaluation of the effectiveness of State agencies may follow a general plan, but depends on local circumstances for its particular flavor.

Viewing the operation of State agencies from the point of view of the common welfare of the taxpayers we might ask if a State agency:

1 Promotes:
— intercampus cooperation;
— efficient use of public resources;
— access to degree programs for all geographic and population centers;
— closing or merger of small, inefficient campuses (see Yarde, 1988);
— good accounting practices;
— long-range planning;
— program review by campuses;
— articulation with secondary schools;
— consultation with campus presidents;
— linkages to campuses by means of internships;
— scholarships on campuses for university students;
— quality in its own staff through appropriate recruitment practices;
— self-study.

2 Discourages:
— programming by out-of-state colleges;
— establishment of new campuses without full, prior review;
— legislative interference on campus;
— double-standards for private and public college initiatives;
— its own intrusions into campus topics;
— growth of its own bureaucracy.

3 Provides:
— access to programs for people who are place-bound;
— a clear mission statement for its own operations;
— sound budget recommendations;
— evidence of understanding urban problems;
— encouragement for State economic growth through program expansion;
— consultants to campuses;
— incentives for wise administration of campuses;
— recognition for differing campus missions;
— education of the general public on the nature of higher education;
— advice to governors and key legislators.

From the mission statement and from the items listed, it should be possible to assess the value and the quality of the State agency's role in higher education. In one sense State agencies are appraised each time they submit a budget recommendation to the governor and the legislature. On the other hand, there are all the other days of the year when campuses and the State agency interact in a routine fashion. It is in the quality evident in those daily contacts that much of the value of the State agency for higher education can be assessed. However, the stakes are high, and the complexity of evaluation should not be underestimated. In California, for example, the university system has grown, according to Newman (1987), from six campuses and a budget of $135m in 1957 to nine campuses and a budget of $4.2 billion in 1987. Assessing the role of State higher education agencies in California, accordingly, is something like studying the entire budget of some nations. Appraisal of the enterprise which represents the interests of people of California, and its efficiency defined in several ways, in higher education is no small undertaking.

In any state there should be provision of a sunset law under which the continuation of a state coordinating agency requires a positive act of affirmation. Formal self-study and correlated review by an independent committee is appropriate. The evaluation committee would include representatives of other state agencies, presidents of colleges overseen by the agency within the State, and representatives of the public at large. A public report with recommendations to State government would be the final, formal stage.

Evaluating Trustees

Institutions of higher education, like many other agencies of society, have boards representing public interests or the interests of key constituencies; in fact people serving on the first principle may also express the second. It is to such bodies that campus presidents and chancellors report, for they are the guardians and that always raises the question of who evaluates the guardians. We start by noting the corporate responsibilities of directors, trustees, overseers and curators. Under charter, and occasionally law or a state's constitution, trustees—to use a generic term—are accountable for the integrity of a campus; they are responsible for the academic and fiscal coherence of a campus, and formerly stood *in loco parentis* as guardians of college students.

In the broadest sense, that of collective responsibility, boards need to be appraised by the quality of their stewardship. That is, we need to know if they are familiar with current issues on campus as propounded by the campus community, but also in terms of broad trends in higher education. Another point is the quality of the person they hire to lead the institution. Two aspects of that topic are the recruitment process and the breadth of input, followed by the quality of the administrator's leadership and management. In that regard, existence of a process to monitor and evaluate the chief administrator from time to time is a sign of quality in a board.

In some respects the functions of a board of trustees are a consequence of the size of the institution. On large campuses with professional schools the sheer size of operations makes detailed grasp by the board an unlikely condition. On the other hand, boards for all sizes of institutions must resist opportunities to meddle in operations. That is not the same as raising policy questions, and boards should attend to such matters. On small campuses trustees may have a personal and intimate knowledge as patrons and alumni. In all instances, however, it is an index of quality that trustees refrain from operational decisions, leaving them to the campus' chief executive officer. We expect to see all agenda items receiving attention from board members, and failure to maintain a balance of attention is a poor performance. Every campus benefits from the views of external reviewers and boards can bring a balanced perspective to consideration of campus issues.

Chapter 6

Testing

The purpose of this chapter is to emphasize an instructional perspective in the broad matter of understanding the impact of the college experience on young people. Banta and Scheider (1988) have described the range of test materials used by faculty in eleven departments of a campus emphasizing assessment, the University of Tennessee at Knoxville. Two departments used only essay examinations and four used only multiple choice items. There are other forms of test items and this chapter addresses some ways to improve local use of instruments to test students' knowledge.

It is a truism that defining purposes is an important first step. In construction of tests for college students it is no less true and may be especially relevant because mature learners are capable of manifesting their acquired knowledge in many ways. One preliminary step is to decide at which point the maximum energy is to be expended. In the case of essays it is clear that reading and scoring is a lengthy business. Time will be invested lightly in the pre-assessment stage, and more heavily at the reading stage. In contrast, a test composed of objectively scored items requires a heavy investment before the students are assessed. In considering this matter we recognize that test-building is time-consuming and that energy will be expended in different styles.

The basic decision, of course, is the set of objectives for developing a test. Some tests are diagnostic — as well as achievement — in orientation. That is, by setting up a question in stages, or a set of sequential questions, we can tell where students' performance breaks down. Another way is to construct possible answers to, for example, a multiple choice item so that they reveal nearly correct solutions, not just wrong answers. We need to decide whether the test items should test knowledge, skills, powers of deduction and powers of expression. Conceivably, all of these and the ability to organize are student skills we wish to appraise in a given subject.

When there are large numbers of students to assess, it becomes necessary to use tests which are machine scoreable. In theory, questions whose answers are recorded and scored objectively can test all the functions we ascribe to essay tests. That level of competence in developing test items is attainable, but not easily.

There are several aspects of test items which merit attention. One is the matter of difficulty of items. A question which has a level of difficulty so high that no one gets it right — 100 per cent difficulty — is not much use; of course there are items which no one fails, but sometimes those can be a first, humorous item, in order to reduce anxiety, and are not scored. A good item is one which the high-scoring students get right and which low-scoring students get wrong. This is the discriminating power of the test item. It is not the same as item difficulty and it is complementary to it. For the entire list of test items we are interested in the internal consistency or reliability of the test. A way to check this is to split the test into two forms composed of odd items and even items. The correlation between the two tells us if the test is internally consistent. Another form of reliability is demonstrated when the test as a whole gives the same score when administered at a later date; this is a form of temporal stability. For both types of reliability there are formulas, and a typical text on tests and measurements will supply them. Generally speaking, a test of few items has less reliability than a longer test.

There remains the matter of content in test items. This is a difficult matter, but it can be made easier if there exists a detailed set of objectives for the course. It is easy to set up items which check mastery of facts, but for college students skills of a higher order than recognizing a date, for example, are called for. For all items and all skills there is the requisite matter of students' reading ability. Tests need to be comprehensible in terms of vocabulary, and they need to be written in simple syntax. A tortured phrasing leads to misperceptions of the point to a question and to failure by students whose anxiety is raised by incomprehensible questions.

It can be useful to discuss some ways to improve the evaluation of individual students' performance through tests, as they take courses one by one in a particular department. To that end, the reader seeking information on ways to improve tests is referred to the appendix. There, is a presentation of ways to improve essay questions and several varieties of short-response test items.

Evaluating Test Results

Once we have samples of student performance we face the question of what to do with them. Good planning will have specified scoring systems and also established the procedures for processing the act of scoring. With individual results in hand we then face the choice of how to use students' scores.

Objectives

One procedure is to compare students' performances with a set of objectives which have been communicated to students. We might ask a student in civil engineering to plan a path between two buildings. Given the pressure which engineers face, and which engineering schools try to convey, the number of minutes to complete the task may be one of the evaluative modes.

Norms

Knowing how other students have done is a way to study results. In this style we draw on norms such as percentiles or standard scores and interpret a student's score in light of the performance of others who have taken the same test. Thus, the student in a section of bright students may be average for the group, but above average for the hundreds of students who took the test in previous semesters.

Criterion-referenced

In some situations, such as a driving test, there may be a criterion for pass or fail. The written portion of driving tests has little to do with judgments made by drivers in traffic, but the State will not issue a license if the applicant's performance is below an arbitrary score.

Subjectivity

Most colleges have programs in the fine arts. Students learn to work in a variety of media and are frequently expected to put on an exhibition as they approach graduation. Music students are expected to give a recital. In the creative and performing arts there is a place for subjectivity as examiners perceive the subtlety of playing, beyond avoiding wrong notes. In studio art the matter of subjectivity also arises. It is more complicated, however, since some types of creative work are personal expressions and do not share the traditional intent to communicate. Both examples are non–intellectual in the formal sense, but also not without cerebral challenge to decipher the aesthetic product.

Oral Examinations

The world uses interviews, a type of oral examination, to make important decisions. Universities use oral examinations quite frequently at the postgraduate level. There, they may be used to tidy–up questions incompletely handled on a written examination and to examine theses and dissertations. In follow–up examinations, professors have at hand the scored written examinations and use oral questions to clear–up ambiguities. Students' fluency is helpful, and non–fluency can be a disadvantage. Even so, examiners feel they can distinguish content from mere verbiage. Whether that is so is a topic for research, and the personal as opposed to content component cannot be dismissed lightly. Some students can explain, describe, justify, list, etc. with ease in a non–interaction situation such as writing at a desk, but freeze up when asked to do the same thing by a professor they perceive as hostile, cold or unpleasant. The oral examination as a way to expand the picture created by written tests is a traditional technique in higher education. The *viva* process of lively questions and answers between a teaching physician and a student at the bedside is a great sharpener of wits and brings information to a state of readiness. Fundamentally, the oral examination is an opportunity for virtuoso performance; but that advantage is balanced by the sheer subjectivity of reactions to people. Developing checklists for the interviewers to use is a way to produce comparable ratings or scores of students' performance.

Grades

A traditional measure of student achievement is the letter grade assigned at the end of a course to a student. It is an interesting measure in the context of evaluating outcomes because it has so many connotations. To the professor assigning them, grades represent points on tests and report the quality of other instructional assignments. Overall, a set of grades describes the quality of a particular set of students and so, as a group, grades may tell something about students, comparatively. When grades are uniformly high it is easy to conclude that high attainment is the reason. That is not a fair conclusion since there may be no discrimination among levels of achievement. It follows that grades are an uncertain criterion for evaluating student performance. We need to know a good deal about the distribution of grades and about performance against previous norms, as the basis for understanding what particular grades tell us about instruction and about achievement.

For individuals, grades connote the level of effectiveness at which a person operates in a given learning context. Some students do not fair well on large, impersonal campuses but are effective students, i.e. better grades, when they enroll on a small campus. While not exactly an index of broad adjustment, grades can be informative about the match of individual and the social context. To graduate and professional schools, grades are a useful index of readiness to undertake serious study. To employers, grades convey a good deal suggesting technical preparation and personal maturity.

Finally, for students, grades can be meaningful recognition of mastery or effort, or the lack of it, with a corresponding degree of satisfaction, strengthened motivation and persistence.

Attitudes

It is a fairly simple task to give a test to students who are about to graduate. In that context we believe that the students' knowledge can be accurately weighed and measured. No less important is the matter of the value which the student attaches to the learning. Attitudes are measurable and can be reached by paper-and-pencil tests. In addition to accessibility, attitudes may be the thing which lasts after facts have eroded. The merit of the college experience should not be confined to what is factual alone, and it is important to assess how students feel, and how they perceive their experiences. Since the day they entered college they have been growing, and the reasons for which they entered college may have evolved to the point of being totally different. Professors present new ideas, and old, family-induced values are challenged by the inevitable newness of things. Equally, valuations mature through life long after dates and formulas have been forgotten; we shall return to this proposition.

An important aspect of attitudes is that they can be influenced by temporary, perhaps transient events. They are unstable and can alter quickly. Attitudes to a current public event can be altered by a dynamic speaker or by a cartoon or TV news item whose graphic portrayal needs no words. Clearly, we are dealing with an aspect of people's value system when we measure attitudes. We are entering into the complex of beliefs and values which expresses the outcomes of their lives to date. If life has been gentle people may be tolerant and liberal but, in any case, our assessment taps the levels of their being, or personality, as shaped by previous decades of living.

Measuring Attitudes

The most common form of attitude is the Likert scale in which we are asked to check whether we *strongly agree, agree, are uncertain or neutral, disagree, or strongly disagree.* Usually a score of five attaches to strongly agree and a one to the opposite extreme. We can score the attitude to anything, including things students have not really thought about ('The janitorial service on the campus is excellent'), and we can add up the scores for several items and so develop a total attitude score.

The next most common scaling technique is that developed by Thurstone. In that technique, the possible attitudes to be chosen are rated initially by informed people. After that, they are assigned a score based on how the experts rated the items. The most favorable score for a response item is, theoretically, eleven, while the lowest is one. The student selects the statement which they consider most correct, without a knowledge of the assigned rating. As with the Likert technique, there is a score for an item, and a score can be calculated for a set of items. The Likert approach is quite transparent to the respondent who can tell whether their own responses are generally positive or negative. In contrast, respondents to Thurstone items see one statement as 'clearly the most accurate', out of their own personality and value system, with no knowledge of the score assigned previously to the choice selected.

An advantage of the Likert rating is that items are handled quickly. They are simple to record on response sheets, and can be machine-scored and recorded. This has always been the case, but now the scoring algorithms can be stored in computers and the entire data set can be manipulated by suitable software packages.

A major item is the question of when to measure attitudes in the careers of college students. To the writer, it is clear that attitudes need to be assessed several times since they are not inherently stable. In the context of assessing the outcomes of the college experience I favor measuring attitudes at the time of graduation and, subsequently, at intervals of five and ten years.

Telephone Surveys

Not every aspect of evaluation in higher education requires face-to-face interviewing. From the one-to-one relationship of the oral exchange we can move to dealing with respondents as groups, through answers they record on paper (achievement tests, etc.), to computer-based questions and answers which require only specific machine-person interaction. Midway along this dimension is human interviewing, but at a distance, by telephone. Virtually everyone has a telephone, and the historical social class bias of fifty years ago can be considered as irrelevant today. As with all techniques there are trade-offs. On the positive side, even small children have learned how to talk on the phone, and distance from the interviewer is no problem. On the negative side, respondents in distant time zones may not be home when the interviewer calls, and the best respondents can hold the telephone to their ear for only so long. The questions best posed are those in which there is no need for the interviewer to scan body language for extra information. Long-distance phoning is economically feasible, and the risk of non-response to mailed questionnaires is eliminated, once the respondent is located.

Logistically, a telephone survey of students at home for the holidays or to alumni in distant cities begins like any other survey of people with preparation of written questions. As with all survey data there are plans to check on the validity of data reported by interviewers and spot checks of live interviews are called for. The sample needs to be specified, and phone numbers rather than addresses are critical. In the writer's eighteen-year prospective longitudinal study (Jordan, 1987b) it has been routine to ask respondents for the name and phone number of someone who will always know their whereabouts. The size of samples is important and can be calculated by recourse to, for example, the monograph developed by Gore and Altman (1982).

In the view of Lavrakas (1987) a critical item in telephone surveys is the recruitment and training of interviewers. With regard to recruitment Lavrakas believes that paid interviews produce better quality data; presumably, pay attracts a pool of applicants from which the better may be chosen, and whose retention and pay are clearly tied to the quality of work produced.

Of course, the matter of remuneration has no bearing on the importance of training, since uniform training is the way to assure uniform results. Clearly, interviewers must learn to conform narrowly to prepared text for asking questions, and they must be willing to report interview items which respondents find difficult to their supervisors. In turn, results of training interviews need to be fed into the text given to interviewers. There are always unexpected matters, and the possibility of refusals, or objections to particular questions requires attention. Trainers need to plan a reasonable number of calls for interviewers and they should monitor the proportion of training interviews leading to wholly completed questionnaires. By the end of the preparatory period, supervisors need to provide enough phones, a schedule of who will use them at particular times and a pleasant and secure place from which to call. While phone calls can be placed from interviewers' homes a central facility provides the opportunity for effective supervision.

Commercial Tests

In recent years the nationwide movement to study the outcomes of higher education has led to development of some novel devices. The Graduate Record Examination (GRE) is a complex of tests used to assess aptitude and achievement for entering graduate school degree programs. From this complex of tests the Graduate Record Examination Board developed 'outcome measures'. Known as the Major Field Achievement Tests these instruments assess knowledge of undergraduates in the following fifteen fields:

Biology	History
Chemistry	Literature in English
Computer Science	Mathematics
Economics	Music
Education	Physics
Engineering	Political Science
Geology	Psychology
	Sociology

Such tests tap specific intellectual functions as well as knowledge. Writing on the role which psychologists can play in evaluation, Eison and Palladino (1988) reported on the structure of the psychology test of the Graduate Record Examination (GRE). They cite a 1984 report by Norman Fredericksen who found that 70 per cent of the GRE psychology test items tapped memory, and 15 per cent measured comprehension; 12 per cent required analytic thinking and 3 per cent drew on students' capacity to evaluate materials. It follows that selection of tests can be a matter of aiming at content, by means of the name of a test, but there exists the opportunity to be analytic within the content about the mental activity evoked by particular questions.

Especially interesting is an instrument developed by the Educational Testing Service. The Academic Profile is a battery of tests which address content and outcomes in three areas, humanities, social sciences and natural sciences. In each content field four functions are examined; they are college-level reading, college-level writing, critical thinking and using mathematical data. The profile yields seven scores each from the list just given. There are three one-hour long equivalent forms of this interesting test of forty-eight items, and the three-hour version of 144 is the sum of the three forms. The results can be used to report group outcomes, and the longest form is recommended, in order to maximize the psychometric reliability of the profile, for individual reports. An interesting aspect is provision for customizing normative reference groups.

The College Outcomes Measurement Program (COMP) of the American College Testing Program also assesses outcomes of general education. A test taking four hours, it consists of fifteen activities drawn from stimulus materials in the world of adult living. The test yields a total score in six outcome areas and in writing and speaking. They are: process areas — communicating, solving problems, and clarifying values; content areas — functioning within social institutions, using science and technology, and using the arts. The unique feature of the COMP test is that the stimulus materials draw on television documentaries, advertisements, music, newscasts, art prints and magazine articles, for example. Written and oral responses are elicited from students. In addition. the COMP approach makes provision for an Activity Inventory taking about ninety minutes, on Assessment of Reasoning and Communicating (two hours), a Writing Skills Assessment (eighty minutes), and Speaking Skills Assessment (thirty minutes).

What is distinctive about these two techniques is that they address the functional outcomes of general education. Equally, they are two quite distinctive approaches and the performance elicited by each creates quite distinctive criterion measures for campuses to consider. An excellent list of approximately thirty-one tests grouped as:

General Education Tests
  —lower division students
  —upper division students
  —all levels of students
Specific Skill Tests
  —lower division students
  —upper division students
  —all levels of students
Subject Matter Competency Tests
  —lower division students
  —upper division students
  —all levels of college students

may be found in Jacobi, Astin and Ayala (1988), together with the names of reference works in which the tests are described and reviewed. The anomaly which faculties face is that curricula tend to be similar across campuses and they have evolved into a general model. On the other hand, the tests just described are very different criteria, and the apposition of generally similar curricula against quite different criteria constitutes an interesting exercise. Given the educational tradition of teaching the criterion series it seems likely that faculties will choose whatever criterion measure makes them look good. In that regard, it is only realistic to keep in mind that the entire topic of evaluation in higher education has an inescapably political aspect, as faculty and administrators seek to present themselves in the best possible light to Boards of Governors and to legislatures.

In that regard, it should be pointed out that the academic–political complex of assessment is dynamic. With the passage of time, we can anticipate that society will become restive from time to time, and attention will fluctuate. Campuses will come to live with assessment and heightened accountability. Boards of trustees and government agencies will learn that some of their requirements are reasonable, while others are more difficult and expensive to accommodate than a simple, direct question might suggest. A picture of how expensive testing students can be has been presented by Ewell and Jones (1985). They estimated annual costs for a small college at almost thirty thousand dollars, and at over one hundred and twenty thousand dollars for a major university.

It may be that some disciplines will come together to develop achievement tests, and that the congruence of curricular goals and commercial tests will increase. Most of all, we can hope that precise measurement of outcomes, to whatever degree is possible, will lead to a degree of tuning of the curriculum for undergraduates. At the same time, an unintended outcome might be an improvement in the articulation process by which students migrate from one level of higher education, such as the community colleges, to another. Acceptance of students seeking to transfer-in, based on performance on achievement tests, would be a welcome replacement for invidious scrutiny of other colleges' courses for adequacy and suitability.

Chapter 7

An Illustrative Study

Introduction

The title of this work includes the word, 'Illustrations'. The reason is that I wish to go beyond presenting topics in this work, and introduce the reader unfamiliar with data and its presentation to some varieties of numerical information. I offer some illustrations of some quantitative ways in which people approach the assessment of outcomes to the reader approaching the topic for the first time. Of course, there are many ways to approach assessment, as the preceding chapters, especially chapter 3, have suggested. In this chapter, my illustrations convey choices, procedures and outcomes in a particular setting at a time when standardized achievement tests of sufficient range were not yet available. In other contexts, other strategies would be appropriate, and there are alternative procedures and analyses which today's reader might choose. Here, we have one person's choice in one context, but in another context, other choices would prevail.

In enquiry of an empirical nature, we seek to reduce error in the firm and stable beliefs we seek to form about the effectiveness of higher education. In data-centered enquiry, the design of studies presents many choices, but all share the intent to reduce error when arriving at conclusions. It should be noted that to approach the question of educational outcomes in an empirical way is itself a choice. We might invoke the historic reputation of an institution and review the list of eminent graduates. We might cite the high reputation of present and past campus presidents, list the names of prominent benefactors and reflect on the reputation of star scholars on campus. Such invocations bespeak quality, it is widely believed. However, the times require more rigorous modes of reaching conclusions, and evidence of a better kind is expected.

In this chapter, I now introduce an example of the process and outcomes of assessing the perception of value which graduates of a doctoral level, research-oriented institution ascribed to their previous experience on campus. I will describe the means and the outcomes of the enquiry, and provide a description of the people who provided the evaluative data.

The purpose is to illustrate the process of assessment. That is, I wish to show evaluative data from students to readers who are unfamiliar with such materials. I provide an abbreviated account of the questionnaire employed, the respondents, and several analyses and commentaries. First, there is a presentation of the method for assessing gains from the higher education experience, and an account of the procedures and four subsets of respondents. That element touches on the design of evaluative studies with a statement of my personal preference; other designs exist and my choice should be understood as a tactical response to a local situation. Other circumstances dictate other choices. I offer some schematic figures to show that graphic rather than statistical displays sometimes are a helpful way to communicate results, for example, figure 3. This is followed by a simple, statistical description of solicited but impromptu comments from students. Beyond that level, we progress to a multivariate analysis intended to show, on the one hand, how much more can be extracted from data while, on the other, demonstrating the limitations imposed by inherent qualities of data obtained from people about their perceptions of value.

In order not to burden readers seeking merely an introduction to the scope and stages of the study, the reader may simply stop in this chapter at any given point in the exposition of levels of analysis, for example, at the stage of graphic display or descriptive, rather than inferential, statistics. Readers interested in a full report are directed to Jordan (1987b).

The task has been to formulate questions which would allow individuals to describe themselves and their perceptions of the college experience. The matter of questions requires that they probe several aspects of the college years. Questions need to be phrased consistently and presented in a uniform manner. Also, it is necessary to present questions which have significance for higher education generally, so that comparisons might be made from campus to campus. Procedurally, the challenge consisted of developing answers to questions applicable to the campus as a whole, while also creating a data set which several campus academic units might draw on to develop their own self-studies.

Problem

Our objective in empirical terms has been to describe how graduates evaluated their college experience. More analytically, we see that graduates as a group consist of individuals who left campus in different years. For that reason, we stratified the target audience by year of graduation into current — 1986 — graduates, and alumni of five- and ten-year vintage, the classes of 1981 and 1976. Our task became to ask: (i) How highly do current, five-year and ten-year graduates rate their campus experience? (ii) To what extent do ratings vary from group to group, i.e. as a function of membership in one of the three graduating classes? We hypothesize that students' positive rating would increase as a function of group membership. That is, we assert that the highest ratings will be found in the group of ten-year graduates, followed by the five-year group, and then the current graduates.

In describing this approach we point out that the matter of gains is not approached substantively. We do not, for example, employ a prospective cohort design in which pre- and post-treatment (course content and processes) change-scores are compared on currically valid tests of achievement with a variety of relevant variables designed as covariates of change. On the other hand, we apply a multiple regression analysis to the self-reported gains. There, the object is to understand what lead alumni to provide the ratings reported. We formulate the analysis at that stage as the search for statistically significant accounts of variance associated with each criterion of perceived gain. By choosing a series of variables describing the respondents we seek to identify what influenced the ratings.

Data

From a review of commercially sponsored, standardized questionnaires we[1] selected Robert Pace's (1983) *College Student Experiences (CSE)* as closest to the objectivs the faculty has set forth for the general education of undergraduates (see table 6). Recently Pace (1987) condensed the content of the gain scores by means of factor analysis. He reported that his CSE instrument consists of five factors he labelled personal/social; science and technology; general education; literature and arts; intellectual skills; and vocational preparation. Among the gains items, the statements about computing have the lowest relationship to other items. In addition, I formulated a series of items of information to be gathered additionally from the respondent or, in the case of grade point average, from the University's Student Information System. The descriptive information was common to all respondents but only some of the CSE items were consistently applicable.

With regard to the question of how much value students attach to

Table 6: Pace CSE items rated by respondents

Item	Topic

1 Vocational training—acquired knowledge and skills applicable to a specific job or type of work.
2 Acquiring background and specialization for further education in some professional, scientific, or scholarly field.
3 Gaining a broad general education about different fields of knowledge.
4 Gaining a range of information that may be relevant to a career.
5 Developing an understanding and enjoyment of art, music, and drama.
6 Broadening your acquaintance and enjoyment of literature.
7 Writing clearly and effectively.
8 Acquiring familiarity with the use of computers.
9 Becoming aware of the different philosophies, cultures, and ways of life.
10 Developing your own values and ethical standards.
11 Understanding yourself—your abilities, interests, and personality.
12 Understanding other people and the ability to get along with different kinds of people.
13 Ability to function as a team member.
14 Developing good health habits and physical fitness.
15 Understanding the nature of science and experimentation.
16 Understanding new scientific and technical developments.
17 Becoming aware of the consequences (benefits/hazards/dangers/values) of new applications in science and technology.
18 Ability to think analytically and logically.
19 Quantitative thinking—understanding probabilities, proportions, etc.
20 Ability to put ideas together, to see relationships, similarities, and differences between ideas.
21 Ability to learn on your own, pursue ideas, and find information you need.
(22 *Overall Gains*)

their campus experience the question arises of who is to answer. There are several choices beginning with the value of recency. In that connection we invited May 1986 (current) recipients of bachelor's degrees to participate. They did so in the period just before and after commencement. Their views have the piquance of the immediate; however, the question of how helpful an experience is may not necessarily be answerable immediately. We would hope that a good curricular diet would be savored, but we also propose that its nutritive value may be appraised some time later. To that end we invited people who graduated five years earlier to participate. However, graduates mature and experience augments their capacity to evaluate and to place things in perspective. Accordingly, we also invited people who graduated ten years ago to participate. The value of alumni surveys is attested to by campuses which emphasize content tests (*In Pursuit...*, 1984). The entire questionnaire was administered in classrooms to senior students several days before commencement in 1986 and by mail to alumni. Stevenson, Walleri and

Japely (1985) point out that bias is low and accuracy is high in mail surveys.

In measurement and evaluation, formulation of the criterion is the critical step. With that dictum in mind we created a criterion of *overall gains* from the college experience by combining the scores of the respondents from twenty-one items to form a twenty-second criterion.

As introduction to the twenty-two criteria to be reported in this *descriptive* portion of the study we may begin by considering figure 3, the criterion created from the twenty-one Pace *CSE* items and labelled, 'Overall gains', in the interest of clarity. In that figure, we demonstrate the information pictorially. A series of vertical blocks describes the mean or average rating given by respondents.

In order to assure accurate interpretation of figure 1 it may be useful to consider the rating system and the phrasing which accompanies each level of the 1–4 scale given there. The average numerical rating, which in theory is 2.5^2 when every option has an equal chance of being selected, means that respondents are between, 'some', and 'quite a bit', both of which are positive evaluations. Only mean ratings close to 1, for example, 1.5 and below, are probably negative, and ratings of 2 to 4 are clearly positive.

Subjects

All people graduating in May 1986 were invited to participate. The PACE *CSE* was mailed to 696 individuals and a follow-up postcard was mailed to non-respondents three weeks later. Two-hundred-and-ninety-eight individuals responded to the initial mailing and to the follow-up (43 per cent).

The Alumni Office provided lists of alumni and questionnaires were mailed to 1226 of them; a reminder was mailed several weeks later. Usable responses were received from 171 five-year – 1981 – graduates (28 per cent) and from 198 ten-year – 1976 – graduates (30 per cent). One-hundred-and-seventeen responses were received after the deadline for data processing. The number of questionnaires yielding usable results was 866. The proportion of females across the four graduation years rises from 43 to 62 per cent, and the proportion of black subjects rises from 2 to 9 per cent.

The three groups of respondents described so far were exposed to campus life for at least four years. In order to provide baseline data, we also took data from classrooms enrolling a high proportion of students at the end of their first year on campus. They represent 199 students with

Figure 3: Means of Estimated Overall Gains from the College Experience

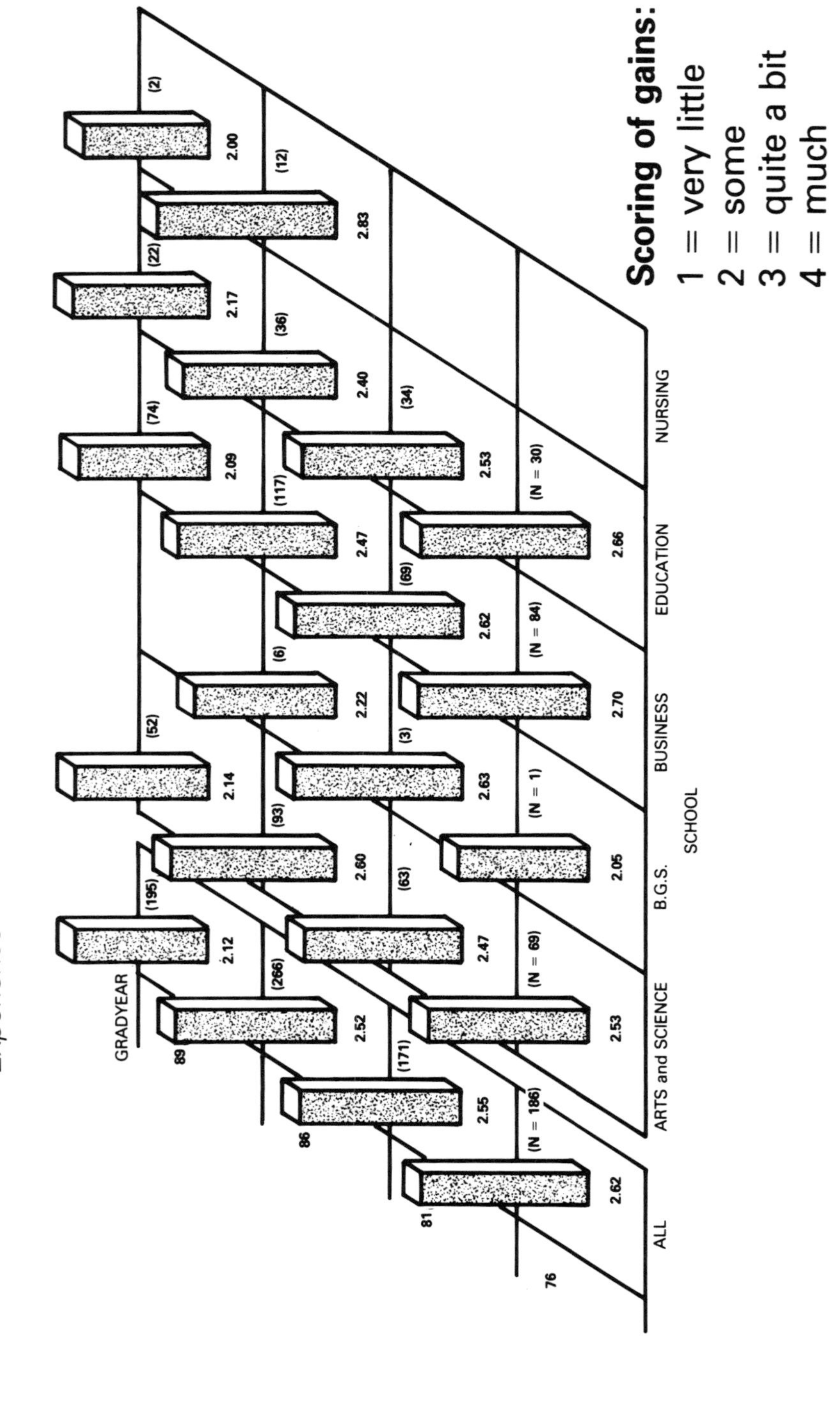

Scoring of gains:
1 = very little
2 = some
3 = quite a bit
4 = much

Table 7:   The number of questionnaires from four groups of respondents

	1981 Graduates		1986 Graduates		1981 Graduates		1976 Graduates		Total	
	N	%	N	%	N	%	N	%	N	%
Target	293		696		600		626		2,215	
Surveyed	293	100	298	43	171	28	187	30	949	43*
Recorded	199**	68	277	93	171	100	187	100	834	88

   theoretical year for first graduates in this group
  *based on graduates only
 **end of second semester students

the lowest level of exposure in years. They were identified and used as a baseline for validating that ratings by alumni constituted any gain whatsoever.

Data Processing

The Pace questionnaire was optically scanned in order to generate the twenty-one item scores plus a total, twenty-second score reported in figure 3. Supplementary items and Pace *CSE* items presented in a questionnaire were combined with the machine-read items to form the data set.

The respondents

For the purposes of this report we give attention initially to the respondents as members of four cohorts, first-year students at the end of the second semester and defined narrowly as at the thirty semester-hour stage of their schooling, and three sets of graduates, the classes, or cohorts, of 1986, 1981 and 1976. Of course, narrower description is possible, and respondents are also affiliated with one of six programs

Table 8:   Respondents in four cohorts and five disciplines

Cohort	% male	% white	Arts and sciences	General studies	Business administration	Education	Optometry	Nursing
1989[1]	38	89	52		74	22	1	2
1986	36	97	93	6	117	36	1	12
1981	37	95	63	3	69	34		
1976	57	98	69	1	84	30		

[1]N.B. Theoretical year for first graduates in this group

or schools labelled, arts and sciences (A&S), Bachelor of General Studies (BGS), business administration, education and nursing. Optometry is excluded, like the graduate school, since there are no baccalaureate graduates.

In tables 8 and 9 we describe the respondents; two groups are small and should be noted. They are the recipients of the degree, Bachelor of General Studies (BGS) and the degree Doctor of Optometry. For consistency, their results are reported in each figure and its attendant text like other, larger sets of respondents. Results from these groups are not sufficient to merit analyses beyond their consideration at a wholly descriptive level. In addition, there were forty-eight respondents whose self-designated affiliation was too imprecise to permit assignment to one of the major groups.

It should be noted that the Bachelor of General Studies program enrolls mature students with unique courses of study. They enroll with backgrounds unlike those of other, younger students, and the role of higher education in their lives is distinctive. That is, they have substantial and lengthy work histories, and what they require of their experience at UM-St Louis is not the same as undergraduates in general. They tend to have narrowly focused objectives, but they are required to meet the general education requirements the campus expects of all students.

In order to scrutinize the data we turn to figure 3's column marked 'all'; there we see that May 1986 BS graduates, regardless of school or major, rated their overall gains on Pace's twenty-one items as 2.52, which is at the theoretical average between 'some' and 'quite a bit'. Respondents who graduated five years before in all fields rated the same items, overall, a little bit higher at 2.55. Those out of school for ten years provided a mean rating of all twenty-one Pace *CSE* items a little higher still at 2.62. The composite ratings by three groups of graduates were materially higher than those of students at the end of their first year of study.

In terms of the six schools and programs with which respondents identify there is a higher rating in all instances from graduates, as opposed to first year students. 1986 nursing graduates reported the most gains from their experience, and graduates of the Bachelor of General Studies provided the lowest ratings. Only for 1981 A&S graduates did ratings decline, although 1976 A&S graduates reported more typical ratings ten years after graduation.

Anomalies in figure 3 are as follows. The absence of BGS first year students is due to the fact that no such identification is possible in the first year on campus. The absence of nursing alumnae for 1981 and 1976 is due to the recency of the BSN (completion) program in that field.

In general, we observe that the years on campus raise ratings above

Table 9: *Description of four sets of alumni*

Variable	1976 (N=180)			1981 (N=166)			1986 (N=260)			All alumni (N=606)		
	M	or %	σ	M	or %	σ	M	or %	σ	M	or %	σ
Sex (M)		0.59			0.37			0.37			0.43	
Race (B)		0.02			0.06			0.04			0.04	
Transfer-in		0.64			0.68			0.66			0.66	
GPA	2.89		0.56	3.06		0.54	3.00		0.54	2.93		0.54
College — Education		0.15			0.20			0.13			0.16	
Business		0.46			0.41			0.44			0.44	
Arts and Science		0.37			0.37			0.35			0.36	
Nursing		0.00			0.00			0.04			0.02	
Pace Items GM	2.63		0.42	2.54		0.48	2.51		0.49	2.55		0.47

those given by first-year students. Uniformly, BS level graduates gave substantially higher ratings. With the exception of A&S graduates the class of 1981 reported higher mean ratings for all criteria than the class of 1986. With the exception of the A&S graduates in the class of 1976, ten-year respondents rated their experience at a still higher level.

In making these comments, we observe that the four cohorts are comparable and refer to table 8. In this regard, it is generally agreed that age and cohort effects are really not a problem (Goldstein, 1979; Jordan, 1980a); accordingly, the general comparability evident in table 8 is reassuring.

Procedurally, we approach gathering data as if it were an end in itself; in some respects this is true, since the logistics of contacting subjects, ordering tests and administering them is demanding. However, research is not gathering data but a complex process in which contacting respondents and testing is an important stage. Once the data are at hand, the questions which shaped the data-taking now assume their original, overriding form; we tackle our questions by analyzing the data.

Descriptive Results

In the example of data presented so far we have illustrated the attitude scores of respondents by graphic means in the form of vertical blocks on a plane. From graphic presentations we can learn much. However, the heights of blocks are only one way to analyze the responses of various groups. Another way is to add simple, descriptive statistics to the materials gathered.[3] In table 10 are frequency counts and percentages for ratings of the impromptu, written comments of alumni. The ratings are listed by level, 0–4, vertically and by year of graduation horizontally. From these simple statistics much can be inferred. We can see that the most frequent score in all three groups of respondents is 3, and that only a handful of comments were unscoreable. The distribution of ratings in both the five- and ten-year alumni were fairly similar, and so were the number of respondents in each. From the data in table 10 we could calculate chi-squared tests to compare the three distributions of ratings with each other and with a theoretical distribution. However, the simple, descriptive statistics convey meaning to most people, and permit common sense observations and inferences.

The old saying that a picture is worth a thousand words is partially true. Figure 4 is a histogram depicting the proportion by percentage of the ratings on the total scores for the Pace twenty-one items. The positive aspect of this illustrative presentation is that we can see the percentages

Table 10: Ratings of satisfaction in alumni unstructured comments

Rating *	All Alumni			1981 Alumni			1976 Alumni		
	f	% *	% **	f	% *	% **	f	% *	% **
0	20	12.1		7	8.5		13	16.0	
1	8	4.9	5.6	7	8.5	9.3	1	1.2	1.5
2	29	17.9	20.2	16	19.5	21.3	13	16.0	19.1
3	96	5.9	67.1	46	56.1	61.3	50	61.7	73.5
4	10	6.1	6.9	6	7.3	8	4	4.9	5.8
	163			82			81		

*0 = unscoreable
 1 = very negative
 2 = negative
 3 = positive
 4 = very positive

* * = omits zero responses

as vertical blocks. In addition, we see a symmetry to the four proportions. The negative aspect is that it would be easy to misinterpret the symmetry of the distribution. That is, we could assume that the symmetry was distributed around the theoretical mean rating. Were that so, and it is not, we would conclude that as many people give positive ratings as gave negatives. In fact, recalling figure 3, the entire set of ratings is above the theoretical center point, and show that the ratings are positive. In figure 4 we have indicated by a broken line the theoretical set of proportions equal to 25 per cent for each value.

We conclude by observing that graphic presentations have the virtue of immediacy of communication, provide we recognize the risk of misinterpretation, which is really oversimplification, and approach graphic presentation sensitive to its risks.

Inferential Results

Up to this point we have seen what descriptive analyses of students' perceptions can show. However, we can do better than that in the form of analyses which permit statistical inferences of a higher order. A multivariate analysis is one in which data are developed so that they can be dissected into components by statistical means. The scores of all respondents on a particular item or test are broken down by associating them with, for example, characteristics of the students. An example is the gender of students, and we might wonder if males' and females' scores are different, and if combinations of characteristics such as gender interact

Figure 4: Proportions of Gains Reported by Seniors (n = 290)

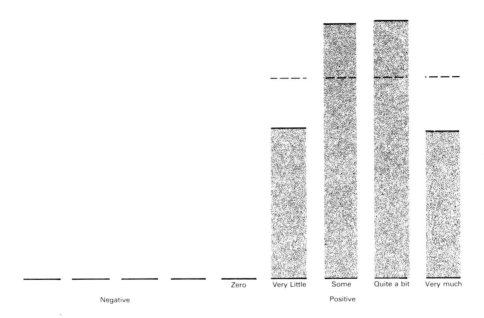

with age. We may also seek to learn if the relationship between gender and age is the same when scores are high and when they are low.

To extend our discussion of evaluation of students' perceptions further we adopt the linear model. The reason is that we posit the college experience as growth through several phases of the life cycle, generically speaking. A rather different model would be econometric in which we would use educational attainment or the perceptions of value received as an output variable to be estimated in light of a state's gross product or budget, with recognition of concepts such as elasticity of some prices involved. Still another conceptual model would be socio–political asking how social class membership affected the degree of power exercised by subgroups who attended college, and who did not.

For students of human development the linear model of variables is generally considered most suitable. Exposition of this premise for selecting a research design is best found in the paper by Werts and Linn (1970). The linear model,

$$Y + a_1x_1 + b_2x_2 + c_3x_3 \ldots + e$$

states that the quantitative criterion Y can be understood as the product of a simple equation of variables, a, b, c . . ., each with its own Beta (regression) weight, plus an error term — e. We expand that model in the fashion of Bottenberg and Ward (1962), and MacNeil, Kelly and MacNeil (1975) from a simple linear regression into multiple linear regression (MLR). In that procedure, the equation given above is augmented by a second model which has been *restricted* by deleting a variable of interest. Both models yield an R^2 statistic of the proportion of criterion variance in Y, above. The drop in the R^2 statistic between the full model and the alternative, restricted, model is appraised by means of the F–statistic and corresponding probability.

Application, in the present instance, consists of designating each criterion — one to twenty-two — as Y (see table 6), and each of five predictor variables as a, b, c, d and e, in twenty-two analyses. The MLR program calculates weights for each variable by the least squares solution and generates the R^2 statistic. The variables chosen for the analyses are, sex (*male*), race (*white*), whether the student transferred to UM–St Louis at any stage (*transfer*), the school or college of enrollment, and the undergraduate grade point average (*GPA*). These variables were chosen as potential predictors, i.e. as sources of criterion variance, in order to analyze the ratings presented.

Model

The five variables in this model simplified for exposition are in a developmental sequence. Gender conveys role behavior socialized in the years of childhood and adolescence. Females tend to be better students, and the alumni we study in this report are members of a generation whose gender-based expectations for achievement may have been affected by alteration in women's self-perceptions and expectations. The oldest females, the graduates of 1976, were probably born around 1954 and spent their early years being socialized into traditional female roles. However, their teens occurred in the turbulent sixties and they entered adulthood in the seventies when female self-consciousness had become fairly well clarified. The younger women, the class of 1986 born around 1964, also shared in the last decade's higher self-valuation and aspirations for women. For this reason, we analyze the three cohorts separately.

Race, like sex stereotyping, is socialization across the developmental span. It connotes acculturation within the family and inculcation of expectations for self-fulfilment and interpersonal style. Indirectly, it arises in the form of the expectations of others, and in the degree of comfort with which the college campus is experienced. Of course, college presents a transition for all young people; a typical campus is implicitly middle-class and white on the one hand, and, in the case of public institutions, probably Protestant, implicitly, in its values, on the other.

The campus has made transfer students, and loses some students to campuses offering programs not available locally. The potential significance of transferring to the campus lies in a possible clarification of personal goals and objectives, but with the explicit risk of discontinuity of the experience in higher education. Each campus has its own local culture with rules and customs that have local significance.

The school, college or program on campus with which a student affiliates is a potential mediating variable in the process of forming a valuation of the college experience. Some colleges and departments attract more students; for example, business is attractive to many young people and the competition in classes is brisk. In the case of recipients of the Bachelor of General Studies degree, for example, the curriculum is closely tailored to personal objectives and so should be a satisfying experience. On the other hand, such a close balance of personal objectives could narrow the curriculum, but it is offset by the campus' general education requirements for graduation. On the other hand, degrees in the business school are in vogue, and competition is keen for access to resources and for grades. Academic distinction is hard to attain in that school, and the pressure placed on themselves by students is considerable. Accordingly, it is valuable to know if specific curricular affiliations influence ratings of gain.

Finally, there is the question of how well students did at their studies by the objective standard of the grade point average (GPA). Faculty assign grades course by course so that the GPA is not a student-generated variable but an external rating of the quality of achievement. It is useful to know if ratings of gain are wholly or partially contingent on the GPA. In addition, the GPA is a cumulative statistic, and it comes at the end of adolescence and early adulthood, the period in which identity is generally settled (Erikson, 1968). It is also at the end of the cycle which begins with sex-specific acculturation in infancy.

Criteria

The criteria are the twenty-two Pace *CSE* mean scores for all alumni listed in table 6.

Subjects

The subjects are members of the three alumni groups treated as a single group. In view of the size of some sub-groups no analysis by major field of study is attempted. However, the design incorporated replication by use of 400 alumni, initially, followed by a second, replicating analysis of each criterion using the *600* cases reported here. This matter appears in table 11.

Table 11 presents a summary of the alumni used to study the first Pace criterion, *Vocational training — acquired knowledge and skills applicable to a specific job or type of work.* We use these subjects to introduce the multiple linear regression analysis in table 12. There, we see five comparisons of the full model of all variables compared with each of five restricted models (models 2–6) from each of which the predictor named in the first column has been deleted. The R^2 or proportion of criterion variance of the full model 1 is given and the significance of the difference of the model 1 R^2 from a model of zero information is given at the end of the top line. Model 2 omitting gender — male is described in the same way. Between the lines for models 1 and 2 is the second line listing the predictor of interest, gender — male. The F-test of the difference in R^2 is given together with the probability of the F-test. The three-line format is repeated for the other four predictors of interest.

For convenience, the details of all twenty-two MLR analyses are

Table 11: Description of the subjects: vocational training criterion (n = 605)

	Male	White	Transfer	Education	Business	Arts & sciences	Nursing	GPA	Criterion
Mean or								2.98	2.66
percentage	44	96	66	16	44	36	2		
Standard deviation								0.55	0.96

Table 12: Multiple linear regression analysis of antecedents to perceived gains in vocational training (n = 605)

Predictor variable	Models compared	R^2	F	P
Gender	Full model 1	0.03		0.005*
			5.05	0.02
	Model 2	0.02		0.02*
Race	Full model 1	0.03		0.005*
			0.01	0.91
	Model 3	0.03		0.002*
Transfer	Full model 1	0.03		0.005*
			1.24	0.26
	Model 4	0.03		0.004*
School	Full model 1	0.03		0.005*
			0.38	0.53
	Model 5	0.03		0.003*
GPA	Full model 1	0.03		0.005*
			0.00	1.00
	Model 6	0.03		0.002

*Significance of the difference from model zero

summarized in table 13. There, we see all twenty-one Pace criteria listed on the left but only the productive MLR analyses are reported. The first observation is that there are statistically significant results in thirteen of the twenty-two analyses, or just over half. The R^2 values are quite low and six of those thirteen analyses involved full models which were not statistically significant from zero. Even when statistically different from a model of zero information the R^2 values in table 13 are quite low; it is the size of the sample i.e. the degrees of freedom, which create the significant statistical level.

In the case of two Pace criteria, 14 and 19, which deal with physical fitness and thinking quantitatively, there are two significant predictors, school-education and GPA, and gender-*male* and race. In the case of gender-*male* for the criterion of thinking quantitatively the beta weight is negative indicating a higher rating from females. In the case of physical fitness it seems likely that the valence associated with the School of Education is due to the responses of physical education students.

In the matter of significant predictors in table 13 the frequencies are, gender = 7, transfer = 1, race = 4, school = 1 and GPA = 2. Gender of alumni is the most frequently observed predictor variable equalling the rest in frequency. In three cases the regression weight for maleness is negative.

Table 13: Statistically significant predictors of twenty-two Pace (CSE) criteria[1,2] (n = 603-608)

	Criterion	R_F^2	P*	R_R^2	P*	F**	P**	Predictor
	All criteria							
1	Vocational training	0.03	0.005	0.02	0.02	5.05		Gender — M[3] (-)
2	Background for speciality	0.04	0.002	0.03	0.004	3.88	0.04	Transfer
3	General education	0.03	0.02	0.02	0.05	4.19	0.04	Race — W
4	Career information							
5	Appreciation of the fine arts	0.02	0.10	0.01	0.44	6.26	0.01	Gender — M
6	Appreciation of literature	0.02	0.11	0.006	0.10	9.11	0.002	Gender — M
7	Writing well							
8	Familiarity with computers							
9	Awareness of cultures	0.01	0.42	0.006	0.80	4.26	0.04	Gender — M
10	Developing values							
11	Self-understanding	0.03	0.004	0.02	0.02	6.63	0.01	Race — W
12	Understanding people							
13	Team player							
14	Physical fitness	0.01	0.26	0.01	0.39	4.43	0.03	School-Education[3]
		0.01	0.26	0.01	0.74	5.68	0.01	GPA
		0.02	0.16	0.01	0.40	4.44	0.03	GPA
15	Understanding science							
16	Understanding technical developments							
17	Understanding hazards in technology	0.02	0.14	0.01	0.43	5.16	0.02	Gender — M
18	Thinking analytically	0.03	0.01	0.02	0.04	5.89	0.01	Race — W
19	Thinking quantitatively	0.03	0.01	0.02	0.05	4.55	0.05	Gender — M[(-)]
		0.03	0.01	0.02	0.04	3.70	0.05	Race — W
20	Putting ideas together							
21	Autonomous learning	0.05	0.0002	0.04	0.0005	3.82	0.05	Gender — M[(-)]

*Significance of the difference from model zero
**Drop in R_F^2 to R_R^2
[1] See table 1 for full titles of Pace (1983) criteria
[2] Regression weights positive unless noted by[(-)]
[3] Replicated

Summarizing the data on alumni ratings in table 13 we observe that the five predictor mini-model did not explain much variance, and the sex of alumni providing ratings on the Pace criteria was the most salient characteristic of the five predictors. In those instances where race was identified, the finding is muted by the low incidence of black respondents. As a developmental model of alumni perceptions the five predictors are unsatisfactory in terms of the full model R^2, the highest of which is 0.05 (no. 21 — autonomous learning).

An item meriting attention is the subscript $_3$ attached to the statistically significant predictors school-education and -nursing. These are predictors which, when analyzed within two sets of data — 400 cases and the 600 reported here, were replicated. This is an interesting observation because no other predictor replicated; that the majority of analyses did not replicate is not surprising given the low R^2 values in the twenty-two regression analyses. On the other hand, it is useful to know that two predictors were replicated in data sets, one of which was 50 per cent larger than the other.

Modelling

In the preceding passage is a set of five variables construed as elements in a developmental sequence. Five variables is, of course, an oversimplification but in this instance, we have selected five variables from an endless number in order to see if it is possible to demonstrate a sense of sequence by statistical means among the variables used in the regression analyses. Put another way, we may ask if there is a statistically derived relationship between the predictor variables at different points in the developmental sequence. In particular, we apply TSAR technique[4] (Jordan, 1980b and 1987b) to schematize the statistically significant antecedent to temporally later variables; the vital connection is made by multiple linear regression models between the last predictor, temporally, and the criterion. One variable includes a set of five categorical elements representing five schools and colleges. There is a linear dependence (MacNeil, Kelly and MacNeil, 1975) among the five school membership vectors which is addressed by deleting one. In view of the small number of BGS alumni the analysis omits graduates of the evening college.

The original criterion is the mean of Pace no. 15 scores for gains in understanding science. In figure 2 is the TSAR schema of Pace no. 15 criterion, the only one of the set of gain criteria in which the critical connection of the last criterion, GPA, to the criterion was statistically

Table 14: TSAR regression models for gains in understanding science (n = 607)

Predictor	Criterion	R_F^2	R_R^2	F	P
GPA	Gain — science	0.02	0.01	4.44	0.03
Sex — $M^{(-)}$	GPA	0.21	0.15	47.81	0.00001
Race — W	GPA	0.21	0.19	18.62	0.00002
Transfer	GPA	0.21	0.20	12.20	0.0005
School — education	GPA	0.21	0.21	4.94	0.02
Sex — $M^{(-)}$	School — education	0.89	0.89	3.96	0.0002
Race — W	School — education	0.89	0.89	15.21	0.0001

$^{(-)}$ = Negative regression weight

significant. The multiple linear regression analyses for figure 5 are shown in table 14.

In figure 5 we see that seven predictors, GPA, transfer status, one school (education), race–W and sex–M, are statistically linked to the criterion. Sex–M has a negative weight in two instances, and *race–white* also appears twice. The entire schema indicates that it is possible to connect the predictor variables describing students across the developmental span to adult attitudes; however, the picture is a modest one. The initial connection of the Pace no. 15 criterion to the immediately preceding GPA variable is the only instance amongst twenty-two criteria of this first vital linkage. In addition the linkage is through a regression model whose R^2 of 0.02 is statistically significant, given the large number of df, but otherwise quite small. In context, the antecedent connections of predictors-turned-criteria to temporally antecedent variables is fairly robust with R^2 values of 0.83 and 0.21. Especially interesting in figure 5 are the indirect pathways of influence for sex–*M* and race–*W*; it seems not unlikely that there could have been a direct link between these two variables and the Pace no. 15 criterion, *Understanding the nature of science and experimentation.* With regard to the two repeated predictors the race–*W* variable merits attention to avoid over-interpretation. The proportion of white subjects in the sample (n = 607) was 96 per cent, and the statistical significance of race–*W* is more a function of the degrees of freedom than of the drop in R^2 which was small. In the case of sex–*M* the regression weight was negative indicating higher scores for females.

In general, TSAR modelling of satisfaction via the Pace criterion has been partially productive for the alumni as a whole. On the other hand, analyses by year of graduation in three sub-groups were unproductive. Of course, the major deficiency lies in the use of five variables to model a broad span of time. It is interesting, however, to see that a determinate view of alumni satisfaction can be generated and tested for a substantial span of human development for graduates of one school using a miniature model.

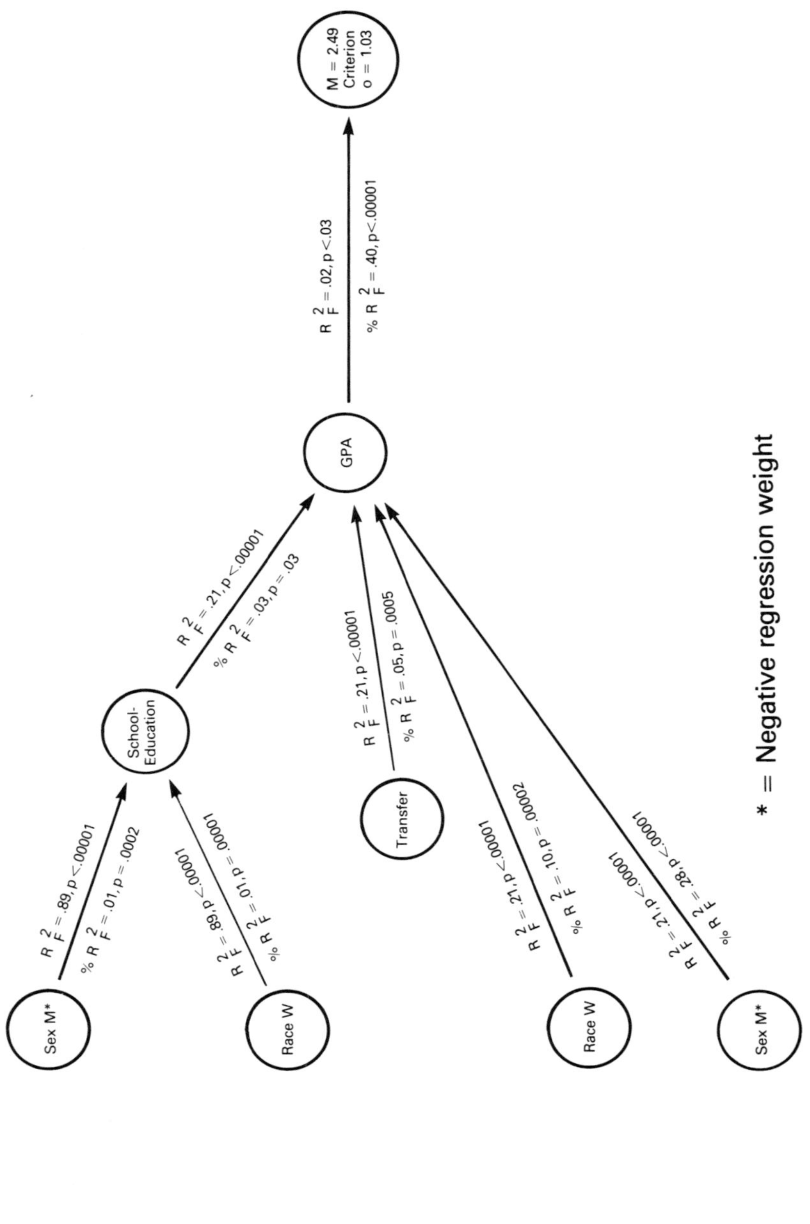

Figure 5: Tsar Schema of Antecedents to Mean Gain Score for Understanding Science Pace no. 15 (n = 607)

Discussion

The design for this study is best described as longitudinal with stratified samples, but not prospective. The intent has been to illustrate over time the effects of a treatment, the college experience. The time period is approximately thirteen years since it includes Freshmen who are, nominally, three years before graduation and alumni up to ten years after graduation. Many students worked part-time so that a minority of those who graduated received degrees four years later. The Freshmen and college seniors were tested while ending their respective year of study; however, the alumni gave retrospective appraisals of their college years five and ten years later. Data taking is the element which makes the term 'combined' suitable for the terminology of time studies. The term describes data-taking which is current for the graduating seniors and Freshmen, but retrospective in the best sense for the classes of 1981 and 1976.

The Freshmen were particularly useful since they demonstrate the validity of the alumni ratings. Had there been no Freshmen 'baseline' data, the validity of the Pace ratings as evidence of gain, of value added, would not have been verified. However, the data in figure 3 show that the scores of three alumni groups, the graduating class of spring 1986 and the alumni of 1981 and 1976, differ from those of the end-of-first-year students. Accordingly, the ratings of the alumni are valid evidence of gain in value ascribed to the college experience.

We open discussion of the findings by recalling the purpose of the inquiry; namely, how much value did alumni from several different classes, 1976, 1981 and 1986 ascribe to their years of undergraduate study? An important element is that the alumni represent three groups five years apart. That sampling procedure allowed us to gauge the impact of the passage of time on perceptions of value. The procedure has been effective since it has revealed increasingly positive ascriptions of value with the passage of time after commencement.

At the same time we note that ascription of value, as opposed to a pre-collegiate, post-collegiate formal measurement of achievement, was the only practical criterion series to invoke. It might be possible to test, pre-collegiate and post-collegiate, knowledge of a given field narrowly defined, for example, American history in the colonial period, but the standard collegiate curriculum is distinctive by its comparative lack of depth and reciprocal breadth. Accordingly, we felt on safe ground in selecting perceptions of personal gain rather than embarking on measuring substantive growth. Another reason is that a time series on substantive achievement from three classes over ten years, 1976, 1981 and 1986, would have been impractical. The likelihood of graduates, scattered across the United States, submitting to achievement testing would be low.

In this chapter, the purpose has been to provide an illustration of some approaches to assessing the effectiveness of the college experience. The study reported describes specific procedures and presents several ways to analyze and report data obtained with the cooperation of students and alumni. Conducting such studies is not easy, especially when a variety of requirements involving tests and questionnaires compete for students' time. In addition, there are substantial costs associated with planning and executing data-based studies of students. The costs rise when commercially prepared achievement tests are used, and also rise as the number of students to be tested and re-tested increases.

Notes

1 Dr L. Sandy MacLean shared the task of reviewing questionnaires and independently concluded that Robert Pace's instrument was most relevant to our campus situation.
2 1–2–3–4/4 = 2.5.
3 For another example, see Boys, C.J. and Kirkland, J. (1988) *Degrees of Success: Career Aspirations and Destinations of College, University and Polytechnic Graduates,* London, Kingsley.
4 Path analysis is an alternate technique.

Chapter 8

Evaluation and Change

One of the axioms of measurement is that assessment is not an end in itself. We evaluate because we wish to know the current state of affairs, but we wish to know that in order to make improvements. Exactly how we wish to improve depends on what we discover. In theory, the process is circular and unending. That is, we should assess and make improvements and then assess the improvements. The practical limitation on this technological proposition is that assessment is expensive requiring lots of people's time and occasionally being disruptive. It is one thing for a professor to test students in a small class with a view to fine-tuning instruction, but it is a logistical exercise to conduct the same enterprise on the scale of several sections. Departmental committees meet and instructors learn, for example, that their emphases are different, and so a common test of achievement is not automatically possible. Accordingly, the still larger matter of using assessment to improve the campus turns out to be a special topic which is demanding and time-consuming. And yet, elaborate assessment procedures which do not suggest changes have yielded only a part of their potential contribution to college life.

Formative Evaluation

It is easy to see students as the focus of evaluation. Campuses exist to serve them, and much of our data comes from testing them. However, a worthwhile and important aspect of measuring student achievement, or the lack of it, arises from the intent to assess the program of instruction. Such evaluation is formative, and we use student-generated data to discern ways to improve the curriculum. It is evident that attention must be paid to test items, but it is also necessary to draw them up based on some settled view of the mental operations we wish to induce through the curriculum. Once that is settled we can engage in formative evaluation designed to improve the curriculum.

Highly student-centered is criterion referenced testing. Here, the objective is to learn how much students know against some fixed expectation of performance. An example would be typing forty-five words per minute. The standard to be reached applies whether other students achieve it or not. Taking an accurate measure of blood pressure and identifying a particular pattern of heart noise are necessary skills which nursing students simply must demonstrate. Non-compliance in criterion-referenced measurement means more practice for the student.

Normative Evaluation

An important aspect of evaluation is comparison with norms or standards. Expressed numerically, norms are statistics derived by administering a test to a carefully formulated group of people; they are individuals who, as a group, represent a significant population, or populations. For the College Student Experiences Questionnaire (Pace, 1987) reported in chapter 7 Pace generated percentages for four groups of institutions. The writer took the percentages for doctoral-granting institutions (DU), which were based on responses from 13,179 students, and derived a mean score based on the 1–4 scoring scale. Table 15 presents the writer's means from Pace's percentages based on the 1–4 scoring scale employed in this study and also employed by Pace. Unfortunately, no standard deviations are available, and so we address similarity of mean ratings and the extent to which study means are higher or lower than the means derived from Pace's data in the test manual.

In table 15 there are sixty-six means from the illustrative data set based on twenty-two ratings of gain from three sets of graduates. In three instances, graduates' mean ratings were virtually identical with Pace's data for doctoral level universities, in thirty cases they were higher and in thirty-three cases they were lower. It may be reasonably concluded that our findings closely resemble Pace's normative group of 13,179 students in their ratings of gains. Within the respondents it is the class of 1981 whose negative ratings (N = 12) most frequently exceed the positive ratings (N = 9); however, the difference from the other two classes of alumni is slight and probably is not meaningful. For all items combined, the mean rating rises in proportion to the number of years since graduation.

Amongst the three classes of graduates the least number of markedly

Table 15: Normative comparison of Pace CSE items

	Item	DU norm	1976	Mean rating class of 1981	1986
	(All Items)	2.53	2.62	2.55	2.52
1	Vocational Training	2.45	2.59	2.38	2.89
2	Background Specialization	2.71	2.33	2.30	2.85
3	Background — Different Fields	2.76	2.10	2.09	2.83
4	Informative . . . Career	2.84	2.31	2.19	3.06
5	Understanding Art, etc.	1.96	3.04	2.92	1.69
6	Acquaintance . . . Literature, etc.	2.06	2.80	2.76	1.94
7	Writing Effectively	2.55	2.41	2.36	2.81
8	Familiarity with Computers	2.08	3.43	3.43	2.22
9	Awareness of Philosophies	2.46	2.59	2.57	2.32
10	Developing Values and Ethics	2.79	2.66	2.50	2.57
11	Understanding Yourself	3.00	2.46	2.27	2.86
12	Understanding Others	2.99	2.44	2.31	2.74
13	Team Member	2.59	2.84	2.71	2.60
14	Developing Health Habits	2.30	3.39	3.31	1.86
15	Understanding Science	2.24	2.93	2.95	1.89
16	Understanding Technology	2.12	3.11	3.11	1.86
17	Consequences of Technology	2.11	3.11	3.15	1.92
18	Ability to Think Logically	2.80	2.09	2.02	2.95
19	Quantitative Thinking	2.48	2.40	2.33	2.71
20	Put Ideas Together	2.88	2.16	2.03	3.01
21	Learn on Your Own	3.09	1.89	1.80	3.30

low ratings is that provided by the class of 1986. They provided low ratings for Pace gain items,

(14) Developing good health habits and physical fitness, and

(15) Understanding the nature of science and experimentation.

The '86 graduates also had the smallest number of markedly high ratings and they were obtained by items,

(3) Gaining a broad general education about different fields of knowledge, and

(4) Gaining a range of information that may be relevant to a career.

For both high and low ratings the word 'markedly' is subjective and appropriate in the absence of standard deviations against which to access means.

By item, the class of '86 also is unlike the other two sets of alumni who graduated in 1981 and 1976. In no instance do their markedly positive or negative ratings match those of the older alumni. For the class of 1986 the items receiving markedly positive ratings were,

(2) Acquiring background and specialization for further education in some professional, scientific or scholarly field, and

(3) Gaining a broad general education about different fields of knowledge.

alumni; the latter resemble each other in the form of markedly higher and lower ratings. Only Pace's Factor II, science and technology, is clearly identifiable and then it is in the direction of lowered ratings.

Suggestions for Curricular Emphases

The twenty-one illustrative Pace items we report are global and so fit some campus units better than others. They are relevant to some academic and vocational fields more than to others. In the last analysis specialists will decide which ratings are important for tuning the curriculum, while others will connect broader criteria to campus' general education requirements. Of course, the two are linked since, for example, business graduates and teachers need to know about the world and its peoples, and both need to be broadly educated. On the other hand, the Pace criteria do not address breadth of travel or competence in a second language. Accordingly, use of the Pace criteria can be helpful, but it is no substitute for campus responsibility to enunciate campus criteria.

As a prescription for change in the curriculum it appears that appreciation of the fine arts is in need of attention. Appreciation of literature, awareness of cultures, analytic and quantitative thinking, understanding science and autonomous learning merit consideration.

For the three major schools, education should consider appreciation of literature, and awareness of cultures, although both might reasonably be considered the responsibility of the general education program of the campus. Familiarity with science is neutral to negative, as is thinking analytically and quantitatively. The challenge of teacher-education, however, is campus-wide, and the elements identified, with the exception of computing and its increased role in elementary and secondary classrooms, may also be components of general education.

In the case of the School of Business Administration appreciation of literature and of cultures merits attention, although these topics are probably the responsibility of the general education program. However, business is an international enterprise and business graduates need to be familiar with the reality of cultures when they begin their careers. Equally important is the negative perception of alumni grasp of science and technology; there is a product in business, and innovative products can be understood through a grasp of science and technology. The School of Business Administration might profitably consider the Pace item no. 18, thinking analytically.

At a different level of analysis there is the attempt to apply multivariate analysis to the data. We have done so, but can report only modest outcomes. The five-predictor set used in the multiple linear regression analysis explained very little criterion variance although some models were statistically significant as a function of the size of the sample. No consistent findings were observed, although females rather than males tended to report gains.

In the matter of modelling the gains reported by using the five-predictor set the results were practically nil. Only for gains in understanding science and technology was it possible to develop a *TSAR* schema involving the predictor sets.

With regard to modelling student satisfaction as a developmental process the results were not encouraging. The small array of five predictor variables in figure 3 yielded a developmental model for only the Pace criterion, *Understanding the nature of science and experimentation*. Grade point average (GPA) was the prime antecedent and it was statistically preceded by the other four variables. The roles of gender and race did not relate directly to the gain criterion but led to the GPA variable directly and also indirectly. The critical element in the modelling procedure was the linkage of GPA, the latest variable in the developmental sequence, and the criterion. It was absent for all but the Pace no. 15 criterion, and no direct linkage of other variables to a criterion was elucidated.

For purposes other than the study of Pace criterion measures it is theoretically possible that the data could shed light on grade point average as a criterion. However, that would draw on only four variables as predictors, which raises the question of the variables one might choose to model a collegiate outcome measure. It seems likely that a model of many variables would, theoretically, generate an R^2 of reasonable proportion, and also explicate a portion of the life span of young people prior to the criterion. Speculation suggests additional variables such as college aptitude scores, personality measures such as self-concept and, N achievement, and family variables such as birth interval, and socio-economic status.

It would also be valuable to gather, routinely, information from college Freshmen about their experiences in the high school years. That is, a college might optimize its impact on young people in terms of general education by surveying their prior exposure to, for example,

Attending the theatre
Visiting an art gallery
Attending a symphony concert
Listening to a poetry reading
Visiting a foreign country
Meeting a foreigner in the US

Seeing a foreign language movie
Visiting a zoo, museum and aquarium
Vacationing in the mountains, by the ocean
Travelling by plane, by train
Visiting a historic site
Attending a major league sport

On the basis of such information the formality of the curriculum could be supplemented by experiences contributing to the general education of young people in their college years. The chief value would be the opportunity to use experience ad hoc as a baseline against which to project the relevance of liberalizing courses. We could set up specific objectives for selecting experiences which students had not experienced. It would make a course in music appreciation more valuable to have seen a symphony orchestra in performance. Evaluation of outcomes, especially of general education, would be more attuned to the before-and-after evaluation of the impact of the curriculum. It should be pointed out that this curricular premise requires a degree of individualization of the college experience, rather than handing out lists of degree requirements. Of course, the notion brings us back to the criterion series and the mission statement, since we have to know what we are trying to do, and for whom.

On small, residential campuses it is theoretically possible to use the experience of all twenty-four hours to educate. To some extent that event occurs anyway, since students live in a campus culture and sleep in it. The rituals of residential life expose students to ideas and opportunities to inculcate selected values, or to allow accidental, peer culture values to prevail. For larger campuses the organizational problems are enormous, but the same choices exist.

For commuter campuses the means of reaching the goals in the mission statement are restricted to the hours students spend on campus. The classroom may be the extent of contact with the institution, except for the library, the registration line and the room where computer terminals are available. In that context, a clear sense that the curriculum must be more than the sum of discrete lectures should prevail. That is, the contacts of the students with the campus through courses and other fleeting connections are opportunities to expose students to the novel and desirable. Frequent evaluations of student perceptions—soundings—are a way to discern if campus life is conveying the lessons espoused by the mission statement. At the same time, we can check on the feasibility of the students espoused in the mission statement. The gap between students' perceptions after several years on campus and the theoretical goals should be narrow. When it is wide we know that adjustments are called for.

Changing the college curriculum, or at least fine-tuning it, is a potential outcome of the assessment of the college experience. The discrepancy between the mission statement and the position of students in their progress towards a degree defines the space in which curriculum change occurs. General education is a major undertaking and its assessment tells us a great deal about the overall condition of graduates. When appraised against the bench-mark of general education as entering Freshmen, and against the mission statement or goals, we learn how far we have brought students. At that point the content goals of general education come into focus, and the range of acceptable courses and electives, can be scrutinized. Goals and outcomes of courses can be changed, and the sum of all changes also can be appraised. Such changes, of course, must be understood in the social context of competing interests, vested interests within departments, and the scramble for resources. However, the times encourage hard choices, and assessment and evaluation procedures are facts of life. The campus choice is to manage evaluation processes rather than have them prescribed, and so yield control to those who care deeply about higher education, but understand it perhaps less sensitively. On the other hand, curriculum change as a result of testing students can be good news to faculty. In Tennessee, according to Banta and Scheider (1988) the state is willing to increase campus budgets by as much as 5 per cent, annually. The criteria are that campuses engage in evaluation and then use the results to assess progress towards goals of student evaluation and to improve programs as indicated by the data.

A final observation on the topic of evaluation and changes is that evaluation without change is pointless. Assessing components of campus life reveals good news as well as bad. Matters requiring attention become an agenda for action and are potential elements in the process of strategic planning. Of course, that means a formal process of identifying resources and of assigning priorities to future corrective action or to new initiatives in courses and curricula. Such processes require time and external bodies and policy makers do not always appreciate the nature of the academic calendar. There simply may be no way to act between June and September due to the absence of faculty. Campus budgets are built according to schedules which operate over one or two years in the future. Some state legislatures, for example, adopt budgets on a two-year cycle. In such states the timing of innovations resulting from assessment can be difficult, in consequence. Even so, the times call for assessment, accountability and change and campuses respond as best they can.

Chapter 9

Epilogue

In this work is a series of topics which constitute the complex in higher education we call measurement and assessment. The tradition of students and scholars meeting in a grove under the Attic sky, and of scholastics bending the syllogism to acquire the art of deduction through Barbara and Celarent has yielded to our current formulations. They extend from modes of vocational training and wholly avocational study in community colleges, to preparation for the learned professions by bright young people in wholly competitive surroundings. The range of modes of education beyond the secondary level is wide; within it students who represent all ages beyond adolescence pursue their own agendas within the context of the missions campuses have formulated for themselves. The sheer scope of the enterprise is enormous since it consists of over three thousand institutions. Each campus represents a historical purpose, religious or secular, elitist or populist, and it has a clientele of active and former students. On any given day there are millions of people buying books, walking across campus and trying to find a place to park. They come, increasingly, from under-represented segments of the population; a majority are female, and a sizeable number are black, Hispanics or Asian, for the first time. The result is a dynamic community busy from early morning until late at night.

Not surprisingly, this complex of vitality consumes resources. Buildings are heated and cooled, faculty and staff get paid and students are readied to enter the next phase of their lives. At the time of writing, shrinkage of birth cohorts and changing demographics have led to self-examination and to scrutiny of the role of this elaborate complex. From a fiscal point of view, it represents an enormous investment in buildings and equipment; in the context of the public philosophy it expresses a faith that education is the sovereign remedy for social ills. To this nexus of hopes and concrete operations the times, the zeitgeist, has brought a call for accountability. The Benthamite cry, echoed eighty years later in Gladstone's Cabinet, has reached our ears. Payment for results is the cry, and we are to show the results.

I believe the results are there to be demonstrated, and this work raises some of the topics incidental to explicating the results we have achieved. It is clear that we have moved from an era in which listing resources and strengths led to self-evident deductions of quality in graduates. What may have appeared as a fad, a transient interest in results, now appears to be on the verge of becoming institutionalized. Incorporation of attention to outcomes by accrediting bodies suggests that assessment of outcomes is here to stay. More pragmatically, the entry of commercial developers of tests conveys that the market place sees a case for investing. Once that player is on the field, institutionalization of assessment will be complete and stable for some time. An analogy is the spate of studies of anxiety in college students once tests of anxiety were available to administer and score conveniently.

On the other hand, I feel obliged to point out the down-side of the outcomes movement. It seems likely that curricula will align themselves to the new implicit criterion series presented by commercial tests. We can expect to see scores on such tests rise as faculties respond to the need to show good outcomes by 'teaching the test', approximately if not literally. In addition, we can expect to see the cultural relativity of such tests assailed, and recall the content of Hirsch's (1987) list of concepts constituting cultural literacy.

In addition, I wish to point to the limitations of data when addressing questions of value. The data presented in chapter 7 for illustrative purposes are fairly representative of studies being carried on around the United States. Those data permit a level of conclusion which is fairly rigorous; however, ratings describe overt valuations, and there are appproaches to valuation which are less accessible. We can simply postulate that college is a good thing and then elaborate that axiom by describing various kinds of good outcomes. We could postulate the opposite, but in either case student data would have little bearing on the final valuation placed on the college experience.

Procedurally, we should see greater attention to assessment of long-rather than merely short-term outcomes, a bias I readily concede. We may hope to see longitudinal data with baseline information founded in student characteristics assessed while in high school, and long-term outcomes assessed in the decades after college. Most of all, there should be a tighter connection between outcomes and fine-tuning the curriculum for undergraduates. The objective is to improve the process of instruction and its content. Giving fewer *A* grades as a sign of rigor—or its reciprocal, more *F* grades — is not good enough. It is acquisition of content and the intellectual power to process it which counts.

Above all, I expect that we will be able to show, conclusively, that higher education represents a sound investment in the individual lives of young people, and some not so young, and in the collective life of the nation. To Robert Lowe's call in the 1860s of 'payment for results', our society in this generation will provide the receipt marked 'payed in full'.

Appendix: Local Achievement Tests

There are several ways to obtain samples of student outcomes and they vary in relevance according to the purposes of assessment; there are also some practical aspects which increase or decrease salience in a particular setting. They include the student's time, the instructor's time, the population we use for comparisons and financial costs. The intersection of these various considerations makes choice of testing procedures a matter of rational choice in a given set of circumstances.

Essay Tests

A good way to prepare a sound and fair question is to write it out — and then prepare a satisfactory answer to it. The model answer becomes the criterion against which students' efforts are compared. From the model answer we can derive a check list of desirable items — names, concepts, references, etc. A difficulty presented by students' essays is the legibility of handwriting. It is hard to get to content when the writing gets in the way. Also, it helps to specify a desirable length so that students have a goal to keep in mind.

Some *strengths* of essay examinations are:

1 We wish to allow breadth of student responses.
2 We wish to encourage development of writing skills.
3 We wish to see exposition of ideas, their organization and skill at composition.

Other aspects are:

4 They are suitable for mature students who can exhibit higher order skill in organizing materials.
5 Chance will not help the ill-prepared student.
6 The right question can bring out the best in students.

Some *weaknesses* of essay examinations are:
1 They require time for reading and scoring; the latter tends to be slighted.
2 Subjectivity of scoring may be excessive.
3 Mastery of content may be hidden by anxiety over the mechanisms of writing.
4 Many students hate to write.
5 Time is needed in the testing period for organizing the content.

Some *suggestions* for effective use are:
1 We should use the essay when we are sure what a good answer looks like.
2 Students should be told in advance what the possible questions are.
3 The instructor should state clearly the importance of spelling and syntax.
4 Reading good essays in class pointing out the virtues.
5 Deciding whether several questions with brief answers are called for, or whether one question of greater scope is appropriate.

True-False Items

This frequently despised item is a practical tool for the assessment of college students' knowledge provided it is used with discrimination. The content is all in the true-false item so that it becomes valuable when testing achievement in the form of facts is vital. While there is room for opinion on which of several outcomes of a war is most important in the long run, there is no such latitude with regard to the accuracy of an equation, the data of an event, or the full name of a person. Equally, the true-false item can only be one or the other, and so the respondent has only one real choice with regard to checking the answer. On the other hand, higher order use of true-false items requires ingenuity, and when used well it can test the power of inductive reasoning. An example would be asking if the last in a series of paired terms is accurate, for example, the past participle of an irregular verb. Occasionally, people believe that a correction formula for guessing is necessary; that view is less firmly held than it used to be.

Some *strengths* of true-false tests are:
1 It is comprehended speedily, and so more content can be covered by several items in a given period of time.
2 It can be applied to information ranging from single to complex.
3 It encourages trying.

4 It can be used to assess outcomes of computation.

5 Many items can be answered in a given period of time for testing.

Some *weaknesses* of true-false tests are:

1 Computations may not be appropriate.

2 Guessing may be encouraged by the 50/50 chance of success on an item.

3 It is easy to frame simple declarative sentences whose syntactical simplicity may be matched by cognitive simplicity, i.e., irrelevance.

4 Items sometimes oversimplify the core content presented.

Some *suggestions* for effective use are:

1 Apply this item selectively to the content proposed for assessment.

2 Avoid in instances where reasoned opinion has a place.

3 Use when a lot of content must be appraised quickly.

4 Write only declarative sentences, positive and negative.

5 Present equal numbers of positive and negative statements.

6 Write both true and false statements and vary usage from time to time.

7 Do not oversimplify the core content presented.

8 Check statements to eliminate dual or triple interpretations of meaning.

9 Keep the length of statements brief to moderate.

10 Test one concept at a time with one item.

11 Use a humorous true-false item as an unusual warm-up to the test (for example, 'A sibling is a young tree').

Multiple Choice Items

With the range of alternative answers the multiple choice test well deserves its popularity. Except for the criticism that it does not require a sample of writing composed on the spot, itself a questionable assignment, this item provides the maximum flexibility for examiner and student. The item, or opening portion, may be short or long, as may be the possible answers. Theoretically, one can test mastery of syntax or style by offering choices to the student. Of course, that is still a passive mode of replying, but the possibility of choosing a style exists in the freedom to formulate several possible answers. For assessing the outcomes of the college experience, the multiple choice item has much to recommend it. The author may frame responses from clearly correct, through ambiguity to total irrelevance. To that the test author may add two more items, the infamous, 'all of the above', and its negative counterpart. Of course, guessing is possible, but the odds are less than the 50–50 of the true-false item. Students know that they can approach items as less and less likely to be the right answer, a process of elimination that speaks well for the processes of reasoning. Also, wording the stem of the item carelessly can lead to correct choices based on syntax.

Some *strengths* of multiple choice items are:

1 Its breadth of application to types of subject matter.
2 The range of ideas which possible access can incorporate.
3 The challenge to reasoning.
4 The demand for reading with care.
5 The call to reason out the irrelevance of the non-true, distracting items.

Some *weaknesses* of multiple choice items are:

1 A good deal of time is needed to develop the stem and answers.
2 It is easy to indicate the right answer by uncritical wording of the right answer in relation to the stem.
3 A one-word right answer may be a synonym.
4 At their best they require a passive assent, not a positive, active statement.
5 They can be squandered on minor details.
6 They are fairly slow items to read, analyze and respond to.

Some *suggestions* for effective use are:

1 Word the stem very carefully to avoid pointing to the right answer.
2 Make sure only one choice is the right answer, and anticipate challenges.
3 Word some stems as questions, others as statements.
4 Incorporate as much content into the stem as possible.
5 Use this type of item to assess reasoning, not recall of facts.
6 Word choices to assess style of phrasing.
7 Be sure possible answers all address the same concept.
8 Keep potential answers brief, and of the same length.

Matching and Completing Forms

These are items for which the student writes one word or phrase or selects one word or phrase. In the case of matching items, the choices are given, and in the case of completion items the missing term may not be supplied. Many people treat these as two wholly separate items but here we concentrate on their common requirement that the student play an active role by providing one or several words. It may be, however, that the step in question is done in an objective manner by indicating a choice for marking by machine or by writing-in a term or phrase. In some respects this is a difficult item to compose since only one expression is determined by the author to be correct; it may be a wholly unexceptionable item such as a technical term or date, but it must be something which students who are high achievers on the total test know unambiguously to be the only correct answer. It helps if such a term has been formally presented as a terminal objective of a course, or as a part of a lexicon of terms in a textbook or course hand-out.

Some *strengths* of matching and completion items are:
1 The requirement for an act by the respondent.
2 An above average level of interest, and can lower anxiety.
3 They are processed fairly quickly.
4 They can cover a wide range of content.
5 There is no inducement to guessing.
6 Numeric answers are well suited to this type of question.

Some *weaknesses* of matching items are:
1 A feel for the author's syntax may lead to the right answer.
2 More than one answer may fit a question.
3 Poorly worded items are open to the charge of content beyond the scope of the curriculum.
4 They do not extend beyond facts into reasoning very easily.

Some *suggestions* for effective use are:
1 Choose the concept or term as important and without acceptable synonyms.
2 Offer more answers than questions.
3 Word items offered as briefly as possible.
4 Avoid indicating the right answer by careless phrasing of the question.
5 List answers in alphabetical or wholly random order.
6 Use this term when the content is difficult or technical.
7 Employ this item as an alternative to true-false items for facts.

Security

The permanent form of tests should be as item-banks. It is fairly easy to type questions into a computer file, with technical information about the degree of difficulty (percentage passing) and degree of discrimination (percentage of people with high/low scores on the whole test who pass and who fail this item) from each administration. For a given administration, the items are typed to form a test. A good test bank will have several types of items addressing the same content.

It is advisable to produce several forms of the same test in order to reduce cheating. The simplest way is to type the test items front to back, and then produce a second version typed back to front. A technically sophisticated test will have all items of the same type together, and will have the same degree of difficulty and discrimination in all forms. This is an expression of reliability in a test; that is, administration of any form will produce the same picture of student performance.

Machine-scoring of answer sheets on which pen or pencil marks are placed is unavoidable when we seek to assess large numbers of students. A benefit of machine-scanned answer sheets is that they facilitate computation of indices of difficulty — how many students got the item right, and of discrimination — a good item should be passed by students who have high scores on the whole set of items, and those having low scores should have failed that item. For this type of test administration the instructions should be clear and the time limits set forth. After the time indicated has passed, students should be advised to be sure they have placed names or numbers on the answer sheets and all lists of questions should be collated.

Sophistication

Virtually all students know how to use objective answer sheets. Standardized achievement tests in elementary and secondary schools introduce students to this technology. The eventual state of interactive computing will probably require less group testing and more individualized assessment procedures. A consequence should be reduction of the anxiety palpable in a large examination room. We are good at testing students, compared to former generations, but we are also effective at raising anxiety to corrosive levels. In consequence, the outcomes we seek to measure are frequently compromised by the anxiety level the act of assessment may produce. It may be less than that of the oral examination conducted by a group of people sitting behind a table, but assessment without the invalidating pressure of anxiety is hard to create. It is for this reason that some tests start with a humorous example or a throw-away item. The goal is to ease the student into the assessment procedure.

Bibliography

The Academic Profile (1987) Princeton, Educational Testing Service.

Accreditation Handbook (1983) Winchester, MA, New England Assocation of Schools and Colleges.

Accreditation Handbook (1984) Seattle, WA, Northwest Association of Schools and Colleges.

ADELMAN, C. (Ed.) (1986) *Assessment in American Higher Education: Issues and Contexts*, Washington, DC, Office of Education.

AKST, G. and HECHT, M. (1981) 'Program-evaluation' in TRILLIN, A.S. (Ed.) *Teaching Basic Skills in College*, San Francisco, CA, Jossey-Bass.

ALEXANDER, L., CLINTON, B. and KEAN, T.H. (Eds) (1986) *Time for Results: The Governor's 1991 Report on Education*, Washington, DC, National Governors' Association.

ALLEN, W.R. (1987) 'Black colleges vs. white colleges: The fork in the road for black students', *Change*, 19, pp. 28–39.

ALVERNO COLLEGE FACULTY (1976a) *Liberal Learning at Alverno College* (rev. 1985), Milwaukee, WI, Alverno Productions.

ALVERNO COLLEGE FACULTY (1976b) *Assessment at Alverno College* (rev. 1985), Milwaukee, WI, Alverno Productions.

AMERICA'S BEST COLLEGES (1988) *U.S. News and World Report*, 10 October.

ASHCROFT, J. (1987) *Time on Task in Missouri Higher Education*, Jefferson City, MO, Office of the Governor.

ASTIN, A.W. (1971) *Predicting Academic Performances in College: Selectivity Data for 2300 American Colleges*, New York, The Free Press.

ASTIN, A. (1976) *Academic Gamesmanship: Student-Oriented Change in Higher Education*, New York, Praeger.

ASTIN, A.W. (1977) *Four Critical Years: Effects of College on Beliefs, Attitudes, and Knowledge*, San Francisco, CA, Jossey-Bass.

ASTIN, A.W. (1984) 'Student involvement: A developmental theory for higher education', *Journal of College Student Personnel*, 25, pp. 297–308.

ASTIN, A.W. (1985) *Achieving Educational Excellence*, San Francisco, CA, Jossey-Bass.

BAKTARI, P. and GRASSO, J.T. (1985) 'An empirical study of new high school and college graduates', wages using alternative labor market models', *Review of Higher Education*, 8, pp. 193–210.

BANTA, T.W. and SCHNEIDER, J.A. (1988) 'Using faculty-developed exit examinations to evaluate academic programs', *Journal of Higher Education*, 59, pp. 69–83.

BARNETT, M.R. (1988) 'Urban public universities: The promise and the peril; *Higher Education and National Affairs*, 4 July.

BENDERSON, A. (1986) 'Higher education: Decline and renewal', *Focus*, Princeton, NJ, Educational Testing Service.

BENNETT, W. J. (1984) *To Reclaim a Legacy: A Report on the Humanities in Higher Education*, Washington, DC, National Endowment for the Humanities.

BENOIT, H. (1987) 'The role of academic program review in university business-interaction', *North Central Association Quarterly*, 61, pp. 497–502.

BLOOM, A. (1987) *The Closing of the American Mind*, New York, Simon and Schuster.

BOK, D. (1986) 'Toward higher learning: The importance of assessing outcomes', *Change*, 18, pp. 18–27.

BOTTENBERG, R. and WARD, J.H. (1962) *Applied Multiple Linear Regression*, Washington, DC, US Department of Commerce.

BOYER, E. L. (1987) *College: The Undergraduate Experience in America*, New York, Harper and Row.

BOYLAN, H.R. (1983) *Is Developmental Education Working? An Analysis of Research*, National Association for Developmental Education.

BRIGGS, A. (1954) *Victorian People*, London, Oldham.

BRINKMAN, P.T. (Ed.) (1987) *Conducting Interinstitutional Comparisons*, San Francisco, CA, Jossey-Bass.

BROOM, D. (1988) 'Enterprising new look at the bard', *The Times*, 8 September.

CARNEGIE FOUNDATION FOR THE ADVANCEMENT OF TEACHING (1986) 'Part-timers: Myths and realities', *Change*, 18, 4, pp. 49–53.

CARTTER, A. (1966) *An Assessment of Quality in Graduate Education*, Washington, DC, American Council on Education.

CAVE, S., NANNEY, S., KOGAN, M. and TREVETT, G. (1988) *The Use of Performance Indicators in Higher Education*, London, Kingsley.

Characteristics of Excellence in Higher Education (1982) Philadelphia, PA, Middle States Association of Colleges and Schools.

CHISM, N.V.N. (Ed.) (1987) *Institutional Responsibilities in the Employment and Education of Teaching Assistants*, Columbus, OH, Ohio State University Center for Teaching Excellence.

CHRIST-JANER, A. (1980) 'Institutional mission in an era of retrenchment', *Liberal Education*, 66, pp. 161–8.

CHUBIN, D.A. (1988) *Educating Scientists and Engineers: Grade School to Grad School*, Washington, DC, Office of Technology Assessment.

College and University Business Administration. Administration Service (1988) Washington, DC, National Association of College and University Business Officers (two volumes).

College Outcomes Measurement Program (1987) Iowa City, IO, American College Testing Program.

CONRAD, C.F. and WILSON, R.F. (1985) *Academic Program Reviews. Institutional Approaches, Expectations and Controversies*, Washington, DC, ERIC Clearing House (report no. 5).

COUNCIL FOR THE ADVANCEMENT OF STANDARDS FOR STUDENT

SERVICES/DEVELOPMENT PROGRAMS (1986) *CAS Standards and Guidelines for Student Services/Development Programs.*

DOLAN, W.P. *(1976) The Ranking Game,* Lincoln, NB, The Nebraska Curriculum Development Center.

EISON, J. and PALLADINO, J. (1988) 'Psychology's assessment role', *APA Monitor,* September.

ERIKSON, E. (1968) *Identity, Youth and Crisis,* New York, Norton.

EWELL, P.T. (Ed.) (1985) *Assessing Educational Outcomes,* New Directions for Educational Research: Issue 47, San Francisco, CA, Jossey-Bass.

EWELL, P.T. (Ed.) (1987a) *Five Year Planning Document,* Kirksville, MO, Northeast Missouri State University.

EWELL, P.T. (1987b) 'Assessment: Where are we?', *Change,* 19, pp. 23–8.

EWELL, P.T. and BOYER, C. M. (1988) 'Acting-out state mandated assessment: Evidence from five states', *Change,* 20, pp. 41–7.

EWELL, P.T. and JONES, D.P. (1985) *The Costs of Assessment,* Boulder, Colorado, National Center for Higher Education Management Systems.

FELDMAN, K.A. (1988) Effective college teaching from the students' and faculty's view: Matched or mismatched priorities', *Research in Higher Education.*

FLEMING, J. (1984) *Blacks in College,* San Francisco, CA, Jossey-Bass.

FOSTER, J.L. (1983) 'American political science departments: Reputation and productivity reconsidered', paper presented to the Southern Political Association.

GIENKE-HOLL, L. *et al* (1985) 'Evaluating college outcomes through alumni studies: Measuring post-college learning and abilities', paper presented to the annual meeting of the American Educational Research Association, Chicago, April.

GILLEY, J.W., FULMER, K.A. and REITHLINGSHOFER, A.J. (1986) *Searching for Academic Excellence: Twenty Colleges and Universities on the Move and their Leaders,* New York, Macmillan.

GOLDSTEIN,H. (1979) 'Age, period and cohort effects — A confounded confusion', *Bulletin in Applied Statistics,* 6, pp. 19–24.

GORE, S.M. and ALTMAN, D.G. (1982) *Statistics in Practice,* London, British Medical Association.

GROBMAN, A. (1988) *Urban State Universities: An Unfinished Urban Agenda,* New York, Praeger.

HANDBOOK OF ACCREDITATION (1988) Oakland, CA, Western Association of Schools and Colleges.

HARCLEROAD, F.F. (1980) *Accreditation: History, Process and Problems,* Washington, DC, American Association for Higher Education.

HARCLEROAD, F. and OSTAR, A.W. (1987) *College and Universities for Change: America's Comprehensive Public State Colleges and Universities,* Lanham, MD, University Press of America.

HARTLE, T.W. (1986) 'The growing interest in measuring the educational achievement of college students', in ADELMAN, C. (Ed.) *Assessment in Higher Education: Issues and Contexts,* Washington, DC, Office of Education.

HAVRAN, M.J. (1987) *Reform and Renewal: Reflections on the Decennial Self-Study Process,* occasional paper series no. 13, Center for the Study of Higher Education, University of Virginia.

Markedly negative ratings, i.e. well below the mean calculated by the writer from Pace's percentiles, were,

(14) Developing good health habits and physical fitness, and

(15) Understanding the nature of science and experimentation.

Similarity in the patterns of markedly positive and negative ratings is evident in the classes of 1981 and 1976. Both are markedly *above* norm on items,

(5) Developing an understanding and enjoyment of art, music and drama, and

(6) Broadening your acquaintance and enjoyment of literature,

(14) Developing good health habits and physical fitness,

(15) Understanding the nature of science and experimentation,

(16) Understanding new scientific and technical developments, and

(17) Becoming aware of the consequences (benefits/hazards/dangers/ values) of new applications in science and technology.

Both classes of alumni are markedly *below* norm on items,

(2) Acquiring background and specialization for further education in some professional, scientific, or scholarly field,

(3) Gaining a broad general education about different fields of knowledge,

(4) Gaining a range of information that may be relevant to a career,

(12) Understanding other people and the ability to get along with different kinds of people,

(20) Ability to put ideas together, to see relationships, similarities, and differences between ideas,

(21) Ability to learn on your own, pursue ideas, and find information you need.

There are four markedly positive and six markedly negative items. Pace (1987) has reported a factor analysis yielding four factors. The items on which the classes of 1976 and 1981 had markedly higher ratings did not coincide with any particular factor. Markedly negative ratings, however, coincided with Pace's Factor II labelled science and technology. This factor is composed of items,

(15) Understanding the nature of science and experimentation,

(16) Understanding new scientific and technical developments, and

(17) Becoming aware of the consequences (benefits/hazards/dangers/ values) of new applications in science and technology.

Normatively speaking, the three sets of alumni provide a composite rating which is exactly at the national norm in the case of the class of 1986. The class of 1981 provided a slightly above average composite rating, and the class of 1976 provided a slightly more superior rating. When disaggregated, the class of 1986 is unlike the two older sets of

HILD, H.N. (Ed.) (1982) *Developmental Learning: Evaluation and Assessment*, National Association for Developmental Education.

HILTON, T. L. and SCHRADER, W.B. (1988) *Pathways to Graduate School: An Empirical Study Based on National Longitudinal Data*, Princeton, NJ, Educational Testing Service.

HIRSCH, E.D. *et al* (1987) *Cultural Literacy: What Every American Needs to Know*, New York, Houghton Mifflin.

HIRSCH, E.D. (1988) 'Cultural literacy: Let's get specific', *NEA Today*, 6, 6, pp. 15–21.

HOGAN, T.D. (1981) 'Faculty research activities and the quality of graduate training', *Journal of Human Resources*, 16, pp. 400–15.

In Pursuit of Degrees with Integrity: A Value-Added Approach to Undergraduate Assessment (1984) Washington, DC, American Association of State Colleges and Universities.

Integrity in the College Curriculum: A Report to the Academic Community (1985) Washington, DC, Association of American Colleges.

JACOBI, M., ASTIN, A. and AYALA, F. (1988) *College Student Outcomes Assessment: A Talent Development Perspective*, Washington, DC, Clearing House on Higher Education and the Association for the Study of Higher Education.

JASCHIK, S. (1985) 'As states weigh "value-added" tests northeast Missouri offers model', *Chronicle of Higher Education*, 2 October.

JONES, L.V., LINDSEY, G., and COGGESHALL, P.H. (Eds) (1982) *An Assessment of Research—Doctorate Programs in the United States*, Washington, DC, National Academy Press.

JORDAN, T.E. (1980a) *Development in the Preschool Years: Birth to Age Five*, New York, Academic Press.

JORDAN, T.E. (1980b) 'Relationship among predictors in longitudinal data: Temporal-sequential analysis—TSAR', *Multiple Linear Regression Viewpoints*, 10, pp. 15–28.

JORDAN, T.E. (1984) 'The St Louis baby study: Theory, practice and findings' in MEDNICK, S.A., HARWAY, M. and FINELLO, K.M. (Eds) *Handbook of Longitudinal Research*, Vol. I, New York, Praeger.

JORDAN, T.E. (1987a) *Victorian Childhood: Themes and Variations*, Albany, NY, State University of New York Press.

JORDAN, T.E. (1987b) 'Modelling causality in longitudinal data by multiple linear regression' in HORVATH, I. (Ed.) *Methodological Problems in Longitudinal Study*, Budapest, Hungarian Academy of Sciences.

JORDAN, T.E. (1987c) *Perceptions of Personal Gain and Added Life-Value from Higher Education at the University of Missouri-St Louis*, St Louis, MO, University of Missouri-St Louis.

KILEY, S. (1988) 'Challenge to get set for the next century', *The Times*, 8 September.

KOMAROVSKY, M. (1985) *Women in College: Shaping New Feminine Identities*, New York, Basic Books.

KUH, D. (1985) 'The case for attendance: The outcomes of higher education', *Journal of College Admissions*, 107, pp. 3–9.

KULIK, C.C., KULIK, J.A. and SCHWALB, B. (1983) 'College programs for high-risk and disadvantaged students: A meta-analysis of findings', *Review of Educational Research*, 53, pp. 397–414.

KUTSCHER, R.E. (1987) 'Overview and implications of the projections to 2000', *Monthly Labor Review*, 110, pp. 3–9.

LAVRAKAS, P.J. (1986) *Telephone Survey Methods: Sampling, Selection and Supervision*, Beverly Hills, CA, Sage Publications.

LEWIS, J.L. (1987) 'Do black students on a white campus value the university's efforts to retain them?', *Journal of College Student Personnel*, 28, pp. 176–7.

LOACKER, G., CROMWELL, L. and O'BRIEN, K. (1986) 'Assessment in higher education: To serve the learner' in ADELMAN, C. (Ed.) *Assessment in American Higher Education: Issues and Contexts* (OR 86–301), Washington, DC, Office of Educational Research and Improvement, US Department of Education, pp. 47–62.

MCCLAIN, C.J. and KRUEGER, D.W. (1985) 'Using outcomes assessment: A case study in institutional change' in EWELL, P.T. (Ed.) *Assessing Educational Outcomes*, San Francisco, CA, Jossey-Bass.

MCLAUGHLIN, G.W. and SMART, J.C. (1987) 'Baccalaureate recipients: Developmental pattern in personal values', *Journal of College Student Personnel*, 28, pp. 162–75.

MACNEIL, K.A., KELLY, F.J. and MACNEIL, J.T. (1975) *Testing Research Hypotheses Through Multiple Linear Regression*, Carbondale, IL, Southern Illinois University Press.

MARION, P.B. and CHEEK, N.K. (1985) 'Relationships between student characteristics and perceived outcomes of a university education', *NACADA Journal*, 5, pp. 53–60.

MAXWELL, M. (1981) *Improving Students' Learning Skills*, San Francisco, CA, Jossey-Bass.

MENTKOWSKI, M. and LOACKER, G. (1985) 'Assessing and validating the outcomes of college' in EWELL, P.T. (Ed.) *Assessing Educational Outcomes*, San Francisco, CA, Jossey-Bass.

MENTKOWSKI, M. (1988) 'Paths to integrity: Educating for personal growth and professional performance' in SRIVASTVA, S. and ASSOCIATES *Executive Integrity: The Search for High Human Values in Organizational Life*, San Francisco, CA, Jossey-Bass, pp. 89–121.

MILLARD, R.M. (1987) 'Assessment, outcomes and cautions', *Accreditation*, 12, 1–2, p. 4.

Mission Review: Foundation for Strategic Planning (1981) Boulder, CO, NCHEMS.

MOONEY, R.L. (1985) *Self-Assessment Guide*, Woodbury, NY, National Association of Educational Buyers.

MORGAN, D. *et al* (1981) 'Reputation and productivity among US public administration and public affairs programs', *Public Administration Review*, 41, pp. 666–73.

NEWMAN, F. (1987) *Choosing Quality: Reducing Conflict Between the State and the University*, Denver, CO, Educational Commission of the States.

NITKO, A.J. (1983) *Educational Tests and Measurement: An Introduction*, New York, Harcourt Brace Jovanovich.

NORRIS, D.M. and POULTON, N.L. (1987) *A Guide for New Planners*, Ann Arbor, MI, Society for College and University Planning.

Open Doors (1988) New York, Institute of International Education.

PACE, R. (1983) *College Student Experiences*, Los Angeles, CA, University of California at Los Angeles, Higher Education Research Institute.

PACE, R. (1987) *CSEQ: Test Manual and Norms*, Los Angeles, CA, University of California at Los Angeles, Higher Education Research Institute.

PASCARELLA, E. (1985) 'The influence of living on campus versus commuting to college on intellectual and interpersonal self-confidence', *Journal of College Student Personnel*, 26, pp. 292–9.

PASCARELLA, E.T., SMART, J.C., ETHINGTON, C.A. and NETTLES, M.T. (1987) 'The influence of college on self-concept: A consideration of race and gender differences', *American Educational Research Journal*, 24, pp. 49–77.

PERLMAN, P. (1979) 'New tools and techniques in university administration', *Educational Record*, 55, pp. 34–42.

PETERSON, M.W. *et al* (1978) *Black Students on White Campuses: The Impact of Increased Black Enrollments*, Ann Arbor, MI, University of Michigan Institute for Social Research.

PIAGET, J. (1972) 'Intellectual development from adolescence to adulthood', *Human Development*, 15, pp. 1–12.

POWELL, J.P. (1985) 'The residues of learning: Autobiographical accounts by graduates of the impact of higher education', *Higher Education*, 14, pp. 127–47.

POWERS, D.R., POWERS, M.F., BETZ, F. and ASLANIAN, C.B. (1988) *Higher Education in Partnership with Industry*, San Francisco, CA, Jossey-Bass.

RAVITCH, D. and FINN, C. (1987) *What Do Our Seventeen Year-Olds Know?*, New York, Harper and Row.

REAMS, B.D. (1986) *University-Industry Partnerships: The Major Legal Issues in Research and Development Agreements*, Westport, CN, Quorum Books.

RENTZ, R.R. (1979) 'Testing and the college degree', *New Directions for Testing and Measurement*, San Francisco, CA, Jossey-Bass.

ROOSE, K.D. and Anderson, C.J. (1970) *A Rating of Graduate Programs*, Washington, DC, American Council on Education.

SEDLACEK, W. and WEBSTER, D. (1978) 'Admission and retention of minority students in large universities', *Journal of College Student Personnel*, 19, pp. 242–8.

SELDIN, P. (1988) *Evaluating and Developing Administrative Performance*, San Francisco, CA, Jossey-Bass.

SKINNER, P. and TAFEL, J. (1986) 'Promoting excellence in undergraduate education in Ohio', *Journal of Higher Education*, 57, pp. 93–105.

SOUTHERN REGIONAL EDUCATIONAL BOARD, COMMISSION FOR EDUCATIONAL QUALITY (1985) 'Access to quality undergraduate education', reprinted in *Chronicle of Higher Education*, 3 July, pp. 9–12.

State Profiles: Financing Public Higher Education 1978 to 1987 (1981) Washington, DC, Research Associates of Washington.

STEVENS, J. and HAMLETT, B. (1983) 'State concerns for learning: Quality and state policy' in WARREN, J.R. (Ed.) *Meeting the New Demand for Standards*, San Francisco, CA, Jossey-Bass.

STEVENSON, M., WALLERI, R.D. and JAPELY, S.M. (1985) 'Designing follow-up studies of graduates and former students' in EWELL. P.T. (Ed.) *Assessing Educational Outcomes*, San Francisco, CA, Jossey-Bass.

STRAUB, C.A. (1987) 'Women's development of autonomy and Chickery's theory', *Journal of College Student Personnel*, 28, pp. 198–205.

TERENZINI, P. and PASCARELLA, G. (1980) 'Student faculty relationships and freshman year outcomes: A further investigation', *Journal of College Student Personnel*, 21, pp. 51–2.

Text of Cheney's 'Report to the President, the Congress, and the American People' on the humanities in America, *Chronicle of Higher Education*, 21 September 1988.

THOMAS, G.E. (1987) 'Black students in US graduate and professional schools in the 1980s: A national and institutional assessment', *Harvard Education Review*, 57, pp. 261–82.

TURNBULL, W.W. (1985) 'Are they learning anything in college?', *Change*, 17, 6, pp. 23–6.

TURNEY, J. (1988) 'Research council probes PhDs', *Times Higher Education Supplement*, 2 September.

TYTLER. D. (1988) 'A degree of Thatcherism', *The Times*, 8 September.

UEHLING, B.S. (1987) 'Accreditation and the institution' in MANNING, T. (Ed.) *Re-Thinking Accreditation: Four Papers for Discussion*, Chicago, IL, North Central Association of Colleges and Schools.

VOBEJDA, B. (1985) 'State test debated to measure college', *Washington Post*, 17 October.

WELCH, C. (1971) *Graduate Education in Religion: A Critical Appraisal*, Missoula, MT, University of Montana Press.

WERTS, C.E. and LINN, R.T. (1970) 'A general linear model for studying growth', *Psychological Bulletin*, 73, pp. 17–22.

'What the public thinks about higher education', *Chronicle of Higher Education*, 2 September 1987, p. 87.

YARDE, R. (1988) 'The rush to cement a union of minds', *Times Higher Education Supplement*, 2 September.

Subject Index

Author Index

Author Index